Living Loved

LIVING LOVED

Knowing Jesus as the Lover of Your Soul

PETER WALLACE

SEABURY BOOKS
An imprint of Church Publishing Incorporated, New York

Some of the anecdotal illustrations in this book are true to life and are included with the permission of the persons involved. All other illustrations are composites of real situations, and any resemblance to people living or dead is coincidental.

Library of Congress Cataloging-in-Publication Data
Wallace, Peter M.
Living loved: knowing Jesus as the lover of your soul / Peter Wallace.
p. cm.
Includes bibliographical references.
ISBN 978-1-59627-065-7 (pbk.)
1. Bible. N.T. John—Devotional use. I. Title.
BS2615.54.W35 2007
242'.5—dc22 2007011263

Printed in the United States of America.

Church Publishing, Incorporated
445 Fifth Avenue
New York, New York 10016

5 4 3 2 1

For Narin, Martha,
my family,
my colleagues at the Alliance for Christian Media,
and my friends, who have generously embodied God's love.

In memory of my loving and beloved parents,
Aldred and Peggy Wallace.

ACKNOWLEDGMENTS

Thanks to:

Cynthia Shattuck and all the wonderful folks
at Church Publishing/Seabury Books;
Rebecca Price, Liz Heaney, and Martha Sterne; *and*
Eugene Peterson, for his masterful Bible translation,
The Message.

CONTENTS

FOREWORD
by Martha Sterne

Not so long ago, I received a present: a small orange plastic box with six buttons on it. I pushed the first button and out came a familiar voice roaring, "DON'T GIVE ME NO BACK TALK, SUCKAH!!" I was entranced. I looked at the box cover, which read "Mr. 'T' in Your Pocket." Great. Just what I need! I pushed another button and out rumbled, "DON'T MAKE ME MAD! GRRRR!!" And then another button, and the famous growl intoned, "QUIT YOUR JIBBER-JABBER!!"

Wow. My mind was racing—how many places can I put this to use? The next time somebody starts whining in a staff meeting, I will push a button and out will come, "SHUT UP, FOOL!" Or maybe at the neighborhood association's annual gathering or the vestry meeting or the checkout line or in the middle of another interminable tussle to get an airline reservation. And just think about the possibilities when I am lost and alone and unsure what to do. How many times throughout the day do I wish I had a strong voice at my side to cut through the foolishness and help me get on with my day with some power and self-respect?

God bless Mr. T, but perhaps there is another way. Peter Wallace offers us a way of life in loving companionship with Christ. In *Living Loved,* Peter is a friend and neighbor with a gentle, experienced voice and a deep, faithful strength who seeks to walk with us day by day alongside the Lover of all our souls.

Peter Wallace invites us to come in from the cold and to "choose to live loved." With the Beloved Disciple, John, as his muse and using Eugene Peterson's ear-catching translation of John's gospel, Peter reminds us that "the Word became flesh and blood and moved into the neighborhood." Peter actually writes like a wise and gentle neighbor, the one who knows your story because he knows his own and loves you anyway because by the grace of God he has learned to love himself. For the great mystery of Christ begins and ends with the most powerful antidote to jibber-jabber in the universe: the astounding good news that we are beloved.

Being loved tends to bring out our best, doesn't it? And that is Peter Wallace's gift to us. Responding to Peterson's evocative phrasing of John's gospel, Peter intertwines voices of faith through the ages—Catherine of Siena, Gerald May, Barbara Brown Taylor, Tom Wright, and others—with his own reactions to living day by day.

In a culture starved for quiet and simple conversation, Peter just simply stops and visits across time and space with the gospel writer and the reader and the people and places of his own life. He describes trying to get through a maze of assistants to a big-shot and reminds us that we have direct access to God. He remembers a family rafting expedition in a drought-reduced river when he has to lug the raft over the rocky, dried-out places. He rejoices in a friend's head-over-heels love affair and agonizes with other friends whose child is lost in drugs. He dips into his childhood storehouse of images and helps us dip into our own. Best of all, he stops and wonders at those thrilling, unexpected moments when the Spirit is speaking to him or through him, when the Spirit guides him on the way into the truth and the life. And if he can recognize the movement of the Holy Spirit, then one thinks, well, I can, too.

Peter Wallace prays right there on the page and invites the reader to prayer—not composed or fancy prayers, but prayers that are simple and honest cries of thanksgiving and contrition and intercession and supplication. He engages us in a gentle, respectful, personal voice that reminds me of Henri Nouwen's. Together with Peter we take the stuff of life and hold it up for the Love of it, offering the human drama to the Lover of our souls in prayer. At the end of the day, isn't that the best gift a friend and neighbor could give?

PRELUDE

Within each soul there is a thirst for love that sometimes feels deeper and broader and more tumultuous than a stormy ocean. At times our lives seem merely to be an ongoing, frantic effort to satisfy that thirst, to quench it with one puny cupful of saltwater after another—through a miserable mix of self-directed efforts to be accepted by others, liked by neighbors, put up with by family members, regarded by friends, kept on by lovers.

Yet these efforts come nowhere close to filling the ocean of need within each heart. Those puny cupfuls of saltwater are actually filled with our tears.

Music's top forty list regularly comprises boisterous anthems and forlorn ballads about the urgent, demanding, unfulfilled need of every human heart, essentially crying, "Love me!" Such songs reflect the desire—reduced to its simplest expression—that consumes and drives each one of us. We all sing the song, sometimes silently, even subconsciously; sometimes furiously until our throats are raw.

Yet we often seek artificial or temporary solutions to our thirst which, like artificially sweetened soda pop, only lead to bad spiritual and emotional health and an even sharper thirst. Or we avoid trying to satisfy that need out of a fear of the unknown.

The actor Dustin Hoffman once spoke about researching autistic behavior for the motion picture *Rain Man*. He discovered that many with autism don't make eye contact and don't want to be touched. But he wanted to know how people with autism really felt, so he tracked down an autistic author and asked her. "She said the one thing she wanted more than anything else in life was for someone to hug her, but the second anyone did, she couldn't bear it."[1] Aren't we often the same in our overwhelming need to be loved? So how can that need be fulfilled? Where can we experience the endless love and acceptance and delight that we all crave? How can we live our lives as those who are fully, wholly, and genuinely *loved*?

Many of us grew up hearing in Sunday school that God loves us perfectly and unconditionally, that God's love satisfies like no other. But somehow this knowledge has become rote, deadened by the realities of life, so that, yes, we *know* Jesus loves us, but we don't *experience* it. Perhaps we confuse it with the world's artificial notions of romance, so our expectations are never met; we live neither in Jesus' love nor out of it. And as a tragic result we aren't letting that love flow through us to others in acts of open-hearted, life-giving service.

But if Jesus loves us so much, if his love is so full, so perfect, so deep as to satiate our thirst for love, . . . then why doesn't it? If what God says is true—and I believe it is—then God longs to lavish divine love on us. If the testimony of John is true, you and I can experience the intimate, personal, blazing love of Jesus. But how?

Why the Gospel of John?

In this book we'll journey through the Gospel of John, the Fourth Gospel, which purportedly reveals the words and works of Christ as seen through the eyes of the disciple who calls himself "the beloved" or "the disciple Jesus loved." Of all the disciples, John seemed closest to the Master. If anyone experienced Jesus' love, John did, and in his gospel we see him reclining close beside Jesus during the Last Supper—a place of acceptance, safety, and love.

The biblical scholar Tom Wright, in *John for Everyone,* singles out that reason when he explains why this gospel is so loved. "It gives the appearance," he writes, "of being written by someone who was a very close friend of Jesus, and who spent the rest of his life mulling over, more and more deeply, what Jesus had done and said and achieved, praying it through from every angle, and helping others to understand it."[2] That is why so many people find the reality of Jesus—a figure of warmth and promise—in the Fourth Gospel.

Over the past several years I have come through a painfully difficult personal time. My faith, my understanding, my very heart have been stretched far beyond what I once thought they could tolerate. I am finally coming to a place of acceptance, but it has been a trying and treacherous journey. Often I have not taken particular steps of that journey well, and caused others pain, even though my intention was only for the best. It started with a desire to experience authentic love—love of God, of others, and possibly most difficult of all, of myself. I yearned to my core for God's acceptance. While struggling with these internal issues over a period of time, often with the help of dear and wise friends and mentors, I happened to read once again the Gospel of John. What struck me most forcefully this time was the gospel writer's audacious self-description sprinkled throughout the gospel as "the one Jesus loved dearly" (John 13:22–25). John considered himself the favorite, the pet, the one loved most above all.

To be honest, that struck a deep reptilian chord of jealousy in me. It just didn't seem fair. Why did this young disciple get to claim that description? After all, he clearly wasn't the most prominent, the smartest, the most considerate, or the boldest of the bunch, at least if you read the other gospels. And yet here he is in the upper room, leaning comfortably, contentedly, on the chest of Jesus, calling himself the "beloved"—and knowing that it was so.

It is not within my purpose—or my ability—to answer scholarly questions about the gospel we call John, but to take the vignettes of the gospel bearing his name and wrestle with them in the light of Christ's love, to strive to understand what it means to be one—even *the* one!—whom Jesus Christ dearly loves. To grasp that experience deeply in our minds and hearts. I've even come to conclude that this disciple may or may not have been loved by Jesus any more than the others. The point is this disciple *thought* he was. He acted as if he was. He assumed it. He believed it. And so he experienced it. And so can we.

Perhaps you, like me, yearn to sense your place in the loving embrace of Jesus—not merely for comfort and wholeness, but for strength and vision to serve. As we see Jesus heal and teach and serve, as we see him relate to his followers and to John, we can learn more about Jesus' love relationship with the Father, and we can begin to understand his love relationship with us. That is my hope in writing this book: that you too come to experience yourself as one whom Jesus loves, even as *the* beloved one. And that you can live your life that way.

Why The Message*?*

In the Scripture quotations that begin each meditation, you may notice something different. Eugene Peterson's translation has managed to recast the entire Bible into a contemporary *koine* English that forces us to take another look at the old familiar verses we've come to know and love. It is not so much a translation of the Bible as what Phyllis Tickle (in her foreword to my last book) has called a "paratranslation"—in other words, "a brilliant lifting up of the spirit and intent of our holy words out of the conventions and sometimes limiting contexts of their times into the becoming and appropriate conventions and idioms of our times."[3]

Peterson's approach is helpful to me because, frankly, one of the continual frustrations I encounter in my own spiritual disciplines is a growing familiarity with the Scripture passages I read. Even though I know that each time I read the Word of God its lively, life-giving truth comes through in new and different ways, depending upon where I happen to be standing in the river of the Spirit at the time, I find I must work hard at actually *reading* rather than skimming the text. Part of the problem for me is that the words of my Bible translation have become too familiar, whereas if I read them in an unfamiliar translation like *The Message* I stand a better chance of taking the time and effort actually to study them, just because they seem new to me.

Those of you for whom the Bible is a more recent addition to your reading list may find the language of a standard translation to be a bit unnatural and confusing, so here again the fresh, conversational style of Peterson's work can open your eyes to new truths. Occasionally Peterson's choice of words (such as Paul's exquisite encouragement to the Romans at the end of his letter to "greet one another with a holy kiss" versus "holy embraces all around!") may jar you or turn you off; it will also force you to pay closer attention and prompt new thoughts and feelings of your own about the Word of God. I think that is the purpose of Scripture, isn't it?

How Can This Book Help You?

This book is written as ninety devotional "vignettes," glimpses of Jesus' love that can be read straight through like any other book or more slowly, one a day over a three-month period. The meditations are divided into three parts.

Part One, "Knowing His Love," asks questions like, Why can't we know Jesus' love more profoundly in our daily life? Why do we have such trouble grasping and accepting the concept of God's loving grace? Why is our relationship with Jesus seemingly separated from our routine life at work and with our family and friends? Why don't we sense Christ's loving, accepting, nurturing embrace of us day by day?

In "Experiencing His Love" we begin with the English mystic William Blake, who wrote, "We are put on earth a little space/That we might learn to bear the beams of love."[4] Christ's love contains both beauty and pain. That means that experiencing his love leads to encountering both; his love has the weight of responsibility. His love must be reckoned with and lived out. His love calls for response, even sacrifice. We will discover what that looks like as we encounter the Scriptures.

Finally, "Sharing His Love" shows us that we cannot contain Christ's love within our hearts. That would be like forcing an ocean's worth of water into a puny cup. As we are filled with the knowledge and experience of Christ's love for us, we are empowered and emboldened to reach out and risk loving and serving others. We become true disciples of Christ, lovers for Jesus' sake, taking up our responsibilities as Christians in a world that desperately needs his unflinching touch. This is where Christ's love takes us.

You are so rarely aware of me,
  how I embrace you as you read the morning paper,
My arms cradle you, my breath is on your hair
  as you listen to the news.
I know your unspoken feelings, for I am closer
    to your heart than
  you are now or ever will be.
I feel your love, screaming out against injustice,
  bleeding, wounded from the pain of others,
  love becomes revulsion when the agony is too much,
The starving children, the hungry homeless,
    the tortured
Innocent, and all the broken, broken hearts.
You cannot bear it, so I must
  almost alone.
I drink up what I can from your love
  in little sips, but I starve, I thirst, and ache for you.

—from an untitled poem by Gerald May[5]

Part One

KNOWING HIS LOVE

one

LOVE EXPRESSED

The Word was first,
 the Word present to God,
God present to the Word.
The Word was God,
 in readiness for God from day one. (John 1:1–2)

Let's say you're in love with someone, and you want to express the love that fills your heart to bursting. You want, somehow, to articulate the immense, mammoth truth that erupts from the core of your soul. Your brain processes those deep, rich, weighty feelings into words and causes your mouth to speak them aloud: "I love you."

Of course, saying those words takes little effort. Turning that love into action is another matter altogether.

In the past few weeks I've been on the receiving end of acts of love from several dear friends. One recent Saturday morning I was awakened by an early package delivery: a gigantic chocolate chip cookie with a note of love and encouragement from two close friends in a distant city. Not long after that, I received an email from a friend who wanted to treat me to an airline ticket to Chicago for a long weekend getaway—just because of love. And I've tried to pass the love along to others.

Actions like these certainly cost time and money and sometimes even risk. But the ultimate expression of true love—the kind of love God has for us—costs much more.

Out of a limitless desire to tell the whole of humanity throughout time "I love you," God the Father sent the Son, Jesus Christ. When Jesus of Nazareth walked the earth, he was God in flesh among us. A human being who ate and drank, who wept and laughed, who spent time with his companions and followers and friends, who slept and prayed and taught and got angry and frustrated and fearful—and yet he was still, always, God.

From the very beginning, Jesus was God: the God who pursues even the forgotten, who welcomes even the unwanted, who loves so much it cost him everything.

You've probably experienced loving gestures from people very close to you, and maybe some of those acts even took your breath away because of their depth or cost. But all that dims when you consider God's incredible, extravagant gesture. God loves you so much he was willing to die to show you the way to true love.

Just as the Word was present to God, and God present to the Word, you can be present to Jesus. You can be alive and alert to God's love, to receive it and to share it. You can be continually conscious of God's presence with you and call to you. You can revel in what was, what is, and what will be forever.

You can choose to live loved.

❋ *Jesus, sometimes it is impossible to comprehend you. Who were you? Who are you? How can I love you? How can I let you love me? I want to know your love continually. I want to live in it and let your love flow through me. Will you help me? I know it starts with understanding your love, accepting it, knowing it to be real in my life. Will you open my eyes to the real you and open my heart to your loving, indwelling presence?*

two

SEE THE LIGHT

Everything was created through him;
  nothing—not one thing!—
  came into being without him.
What came into existence was Life,
  and the Life was Light to live by.

The Light-Life blazed out of the darkness;
the darkness couldn't put it out. (John 1:3–5)

Jesus blazes with love. For you. He created you. His fingerprints are all over you. His heart is interwoven with your heart; his love infuses your every cell. He is the source, the creator, of your life—your very existence.

Jesus lived in such a way as to shine the light of love into every dark corner, including the dark corners of every heart. His love blazes brightly into the darkness in which we huddle for presumed safety.

If we want to live in his love, we will go to him as our source—our only source—for life. For light. For love.

We'll stop trying to fill all the open sores in our heart with the world's quick-fix spackle of fake relationships or meaningless sex or mind-numbing activities or other useless, soul-damaging pursuits. We'll stop shoving our genuine, desperate needs into our dark unconscious, where we think they are safely tucked away, but where they fester like rotten garbage in a forgotten corner under the kitchen sink. We'll stop inflating our hearts, our egos, and our hopes through our own meaningless accomplishments, our own silly, temporary solutions. We'll stop avoiding facing our fears and inadequacies and pains and weaknesses because we feel so powerless against them.

We'll stop all that—and start looking to the Light that gives life, the Light of love that heals our open sores, fills our needs, and gives us hope and strength and wisdom for living.

Know this: Your life begins and ends with Jesus. His love surrounds you and upholds you. It seeks to fill you and steady you. You can go through life oblivious to his love; you can go off on your own. Or, like John, you can stick close to the one who knows you inside-out, so you can sense his steady, sure, loving embrace.

Open your heart to the source of all life and love. Open your darkness to the Light.

❋ *Jesus, I am tired of living my life outside your loving embrace. I am weary of trying to fix things my way or of ignoring the fact that things are even broken to start with. I am done fighting against the relentless gravity of the truth that you, and you alone, are my Life. You are my Light. You are my Love. Open my eyes and my heart to you even more today.*

three

WANTING THE REAL THING

The Life-Light was the real thing:
  Every person entering Life
  he brings into Light.
He was in the world,
  the world was there through him,
  and yet the world didn't even notice.
He came to his own people,
  but they didn't want him.
But whoever did want him,
  who believed he was who he claimed
  and would do what he said,
He made to be their true selves,
  their child-of-God selves.
These are the God-begotten,
  not blood-begotten,
  not flesh-begotten,
  not sex-begotten. (John 1:9–13)

Picture this: A beautiful young woman stubbornly resisting the love of numerous family members and friends, caught in the grip of addiction and sin. As a result, she has lost her job, her home, even her child. Her loved ones pray for her relentlessly, try to reach out to her; they offer to help her, but she resists.

Maybe it's her sense of humiliation that keeps her back turned to the love that reaches for her. Maybe her feelings of guilt keep her walled up. Maybe fear of what will happen next keeps her from answering her loved ones' phone calls. Maybe she's so caught up in her problems that she can't even see what's waiting for her: help and hope and unbounded love.

Each one of us has, at one time or another, been in a similar place as this young woman. Jesus, God in the flesh, walked on this very planet, which he created. He lived in this same world. He came to be with us, the people he had made.

But they—we—rejected him.

We were blind to his light. We turned our back on our Creator. We refused his love.

Today each of us faces a choice, and it is a matter of life and death: *Do I want to be in relationship with this God-man? Do I want Jesus?*

John, the disciple Jesus loved, believed that his master, with whom he lived 24/7, was the real thing. In the passage above he makes a promise that's rich with possibilities: If you want Jesus, if you believe he is who he claimed to be, if you follow after him and live within his embrace, Jesus will make you to be your true self. Your child-of-God self. Fully realized, fully engaged, fully beloved.

And you, like Jesus himself, will be "God-begotten." You will be just as precious and loved of the Father as Jesus himself was.

Those who don't want Jesus betray their true selves because they will never experience all the joy and meaning and purpose, all the thrill of living, all the light of love that Jesus created us to know and experience and share.

Choose to want Jesus. Choose to live loved. I get a sense that beautiful young woman finally is.

❋ *Jesus, the choice seems so simple. Why would I not want you? Yet, when I'm honest, I realize I betray you every day, every moment, through my actions and inactions. I choose now to receive your love, to live loved. Give me the wisdom and strength to make this choice every day. And to be open to whatever happens as a result.*

four

WITH YOUR OWN EYES

The Word became flesh and blood,
 and moved into the neighborhood.
We saw the glory with our own eyes,
 the one-of-a-kind glory,
 like Father, like Son,
Generous inside and out,
 true from start to finish. (John 1:14)

Why do we fear love? Maybe because we've all been hurt in our pursuit of it. We know what it feels like to meet someone—a potential friend or even a life partner—and feel the spark of mutual interest. Our hopes arise: *Maybe this person will be the one. Finally, someone who really enjoys me and wants to share my company, someone who will give me love and receive mine in return, in healthy mutuality. Love with no strings and no limits.*

But before long, our hopes dim as the person's true colors are revealed. Why, this "friend" is even more selfish than we are! Disappointed once again, we get up and move on, looking for the next candidate to try to meet our immense need for love and acceptance.

According to John, we don't need to look any further. Jesus has "moved into the neighborhood." John vouches for this Word-become-flesh-and-blood. With his own eyes, every day for three years, John saw Jesus live and teach and work miracles. He saw Jesus tired and hungry and angry and homesick for heaven. He realized that Jesus was unique, sent from above. John learned firsthand what Jesus' true colors were: he was generous with love and wisdom, totally trustworthy, honest, and real.

So why be afraid of the love Jesus offers you? It has already been tested and found solid and secure. He has proven his real love, time and time again. Now he wants to prove it to you.

What if you lived like you believed that? Perhaps you would make that extra effort to spend time with him in prayer, to worship with those who share the same love, to reach out to those who are sick and lonely and haven't yet met Jesus.

Jesus is with you now. He's ready to help you to find out for yourself what life will be like when you live loved.

❋ *Jesus, thank you for coming to live among us, to be right here with me. Help me to know you, to see you with my own eyes—your glory, your generosity, your truth, and your love. Dissolve my fear of loving you, my fear of risking my heart that has been broken far too many times. Are you for real? Let me find out today.*

five

PLAIN AS DAY

No one has ever seen God,
  not so much as a glimpse.
This one-of-a-kind God-Expression,
  who exists at the very heart of the Father,
  has made him plain as day. (John 1:18)

How do we get our minds around this God who loves us so much? After all, we can't put our arms around him. We can't see him with our eyes or feel him with our hands. When it comes to knowing and understanding God, I often feel like that poor student with the tiny head in the Gary Larson "Far Side" cartoon, who pathetically complains to his teacher that his brain is full.

God can seem like an overwhelming abstract principle. A detached observer. A mysterious behind-the-scenes director. Some of us even struggle to believe in this unseen God.

Yes, the Bible gives us account after account of God's miraculous work throughout history. It spells out all the divine principles and commands and wisdom for living. But as much as we revere the Bible, it too is hard to grasp and to put to work in our lives in any coherent, consistent way. The Bible seems so radical and overwhelming; it's impossible to obey every jot and tittle. So, not only do our brains feel full, but our hearts feel far too tiny.

God knew we would struggle with this, and love prompted God to approach us, to reach out to us by sending Jesus into the world to show us more clearly who God is. Jesus was unique: a fully divine, fully human expression of everything God is and everything God intended human life to be.

So, by watching Jesus confront injustice boldly, reach out to sinful men and women unreservedly, challenge faithlessness with burning passion, share love and acceptance with breath-taking liberality, we can see what God is all about. Jesus "exists at the very heart of the Father." Jesus is close beside the Father, intimately and lovingly present. And Jesus invites you to join him there.

Put aside, if you can, all your presuppositions about God, all your true and all your false pictures of what the Father looks like, all your understandings and misunderstandings about what God is about.

Come close to Jesus and see God plain as day.

❋ *Jesus, I feel the need to start fresh and learn about God by being in your loving presence, by seeing how you lived and loved, by coming to know you intimately. Help me to be open to seeing God by seeing you and knowing you and loving you.*

six

CLEAN AND READY

The very next day John saw Jesus coming toward him and yelled out, "Here he is, God's Passover Lamb! He forgives the sins of the world! This is the man I've been talking about, 'the One who comes after me but is really ahead of me.' I

> knew nothing about who he was—only this: that my task has been to get Israel ready to recognize him as the God-Revealer. That is why I came here baptizing with water, giving you a good bath and scrubbing sins from your life so you can get a fresh start with God." (John 1:29–31)

John the Baptizer was clear about his role. God had sent him to point the way to the Life-Light, Jesus, the Word. He had come to "thunder in the desert: 'Make the road straight for God!'"(1:23).

So, when Jesus was ready to begin his ministry, to reveal himself to the world and to express God's love in tangible ways, this John was eager to shout out the good news. If God's people were to discover their true identity as God's beloved, they had to be ready for it. So John the Baptizer had come to prepare people to open their eyes, their minds, and their hearts to a new way of life.

Wild John had come to help each willing person to get scrubbed clean from the wrong ways they'd lived, so they would be ready to start fresh on a new path of love. He had come to describe God's Passover Lamb, so each person would recognize him for who he is: the God-Revealer. The Sin-Bearer. The Love-Expresser.

Just as Israel required preparation for the entry of the Lamb, so do we.

In order to know Jesus' love, to experience his life-giving presence, we need to be clean and ready. We need to be cleansed of our wrong-headed thinking, our false starts, our spiritual blindness, and our fruitless, frantic efforts to soothe our own souls. We need a good bath in the freeing, filling waters of the Spirit, so we can start fresh with God.

What does that mean for you? Do you have negative relationships that you need to let go of? Any harmful habits to release? Any false assumptions and erroneous expectations about life you need to let the Spirit dissolve? Any prejudices you like to call "values" that you need to have washed away?

This can be excruciatingly difficult, because even though they're harmful to us, we have come to nurse and even cherish such things. It took me years and years to open my clenched hands in a major area of my life, so Jesus could take away the false hopes and self-protective notions I grasped with every ounce of energy. But when my grip loosened, when I let him clean me of my pitiful efforts at doing good and being right, then I could start fresh with him. The road ahead is long, but at least now I sense I am heading in the right direction.

John the Baptizer is calling to you, pointing the way to cleansing and to new life. Do you hear him?

❋ *Jesus, bathe me in the cleansing, sin-dissolving Spirit. Thank you for forgiving my sins, for making me new, for making the crooked, rough road of my heart straight and sure, ready for your coming into my life. I am ready.*

seven

WHAT ARE YOU AFTER?

> The next day John was back at his post with two disciples, who were watching. He looked up, saw Jesus walking nearby, and said, "Here he is, God's Passover Lamb."
>
> The two disciples heard him and went after Jesus. Jesus looked over his shoulder and said to them, "What are you after?"
>
> They said, "Rabbi" (which means "Teacher"), "where are you staying?"
>
> He replied, "Come along and see for yourself."
>
> (John 1:35–39)

When two of John the Baptizer's disciples hear him call Jesus "God's Passover Lamb," the one who is the way of salvation, they immediately follow him. Literally.

Quietly these two men—Andrew and, many suspect, John—walk behind Jesus, no doubt nervous and excited, confused, a little unsure what to do next, their minds racing with questions. Jesus senses their hovering presence, turns around, and asks them directly, "What are you after?"

They honor him by calling him Teacher, but they aren't sure how to respond. What do they want from him? Why are they following him? Do they even know who he is? So they blurt out a question: "Where are you staying?"

They just want to be with Jesus, to see where he lived, to spend a day with him, listening to him, learning his purposes, his goals, his heart. They want to get to know him.

Jesus warmly invites them to "come along and see for yourself." It's a simple answer, but one brimming with possibilities and promise because he is inviting them to be with him on an intimate level. So they spend the day with Jesus, and in those few hours they become his committed followers and faithful friends.

Wouldn't you have loved to be with the two disciples as they went with Jesus for the day?

Their mentor, John the Baptizer, had pointed Jesus out as the one whom God had sent to express love, mercy, and forgiveness to the world. So they went after him.

Jesus is direct in his question. It's a question he still asks us today: "What are you after?"

- Are you looking for clear answers to life's most challenging questions?
- Are you looking for a set of rules to follow diligently in order to receive God's (or perhaps some religious leader's) approval?
- Are you looking for a miracle to revolutionize your dreary life, to fix all your problems, to make things right—at least as *you* define right?
- Are you looking for a divine anesthesia for the pains and problems that continually vex you, that weary your bones and shrivel your heart?
- Are you looking for abundant blessings? Political power? Worldly success? Material prosperity?

The disciples didn't want any of these things. All they wanted was Jesus' company. They just wanted to be with him, to learn from him, to experience him. And they got what they wanted. For the next three years and beyond, they would get a lot more than they could ever have imagined. They would be stretched to the limit in discovering the amount of love and pain and joy and fear and strength and purpose they could bear.

If you want to experience Jesus' loving presence, his words to you are the same as his words to these disciples: "Come along and see for yourself."

What do you want from Jesus? And are you prepared to receive it?

✻ *Jesus, I get so confused about my motives, my desires, my purposes in wanting to know you and follow you. Help me to get clear in my mind what I want from you, and reveal to me what you want from me. To do that, I want simply to be with you, just for the day, so you can prepare me for what's to come.*

eight

A LOVER'S NAME

Andrew, Simon Peter's brother, was one of the two who heard John's witness and followed Jesus. The first thing he did after finding where Jesus lived was find his own brother, Simon, telling him, "We've found the Messiah" (that is, "Christ"). He immediately led him to Jesus.

Jesus took one look up and said, "You're John's son, Simon? From now on your name is Cephas" (or Peter, which means "Rock"). (John 1:40–42)

When we come to Jesus to get to know him, we find he already knows us. Thoroughly. Inside and out. He knows us well enough to give us a special new name, one that both captures our personality and prophesies our destiny.

He did that with Simon, Andrew's brother. Andrew, along with another disciple (John the beloved, most likely), had spent a day with Jesus, and Andrew found his heart taken captive by the man. Immediately, Andrew brought Simon to the one he was convinced was the long-awaited Messiah.

Jesus took one look and sized up Simon: the rough, tough exterior, the inner strength, perhaps even the propensity to crack under pressure—and he called him "the Rock." I love this story because it reminds me of my Dad greeting me excitedly when I was a little boy with his favorite nickname for me: "Rocky!"

If Jesus were to give you a new name, what do you think it would be?

In the letter to the Christians at Pergamum, which many believe Jesus dictated to John much later, he makes a promise: "I'll also give a clear, smooth stone inscribed with your new name, your secret new name" (Revelation 2:17).

That sounds to me like Jesus has already given each of us a new name. He's come up with a pet name for each of us. A name like one a lover has with his beloved, a name only they share. A name that both captures and releases us at the same moment.

So, what does Jesus call you? Have you heard him speak your name? Have you heard his quiet whisper beckoning you into his loving presence? It's probably not audible, really. But your heart can hear it. It comes in those moments when you find yourself far too self-absorbed, covered by work or worry, losing hope in the face of chaos or tragedy. In those times, you sense Jesus' spirit pulling you aside, inviting you to stop running scared and instead settle into his arms and, as we say in the South, let him love on you.

If you don't know your nickname yet, you will someday. In the meantime, keep spending time with your Lord, keep learning how to love him, and keep listening for Jesus' loving whisper to you.

❋ *Jesus, it both scares me and strengthens me that you know me so well, so thoroughly. It scares me because it means you know everything about me—my gross thoughts, my selfish actions, my weak faith. And yet it strengthens me because despite all that, I know you are still with me. You still call me by name. You still whisper your love to me. Thank you.*

nine SURPRISING REALITIES

> The next day Jesus decided to go to Galilee. When he got there, he ran across Philip and said, "Come, follow me." (Philip's hometown was Bethsaida, the same as Andrew and Peter.)
>
> Philip went and found Nathanael and told him, "We've found the One Moses wrote of in the Law, the One preached by the prophets. It's *Jesus,* Joseph's son, the one from Nazareth!" Nathanael said, "Nazareth? You've got to be kidding."
>
> But Philip said, "Come, see for yourself." (John 1:43–46)

Some people think they have already figured Jesus out. They reduce him to a series of facts, a list of rules. They, in effect, put him in a box. So they don't expect him to act the way he sometimes does.

Look ahead in John's gospel and consider the time he walks on the surface of the lake toward his terrified friends. Or the time he erupts in fury at the merchants inside God's temple. Or the many people hurting for so many years whom, with a simple touch, he sets free from their diseases. Or the many times he overturns the rationalizations of very religious people. Jesus would soon become known as someone who acted well outside the box.

Of course, none of those events had taken place when Nathanael met Jesus. Maybe that's why it made absolutely no sense to him that the one for whom he and the nation of Israel had waited for centuries, the Messiah, would come from Nazareth—a village just up the road from Cana, Nathanael's hometown. What sort of triumphant king would come from that Podunk place to rule Israel? Nothing good comes out of Nazareth!

As Nathanael would discover, Jesus is full of surprises. Throughout the gospel accounts, Jesus continually baffled both his closest friends and his bitterest enemies.

Getting to know Jesus means learning to expect the unexpected. Just when we think we have him all figured out, he does something we never saw coming. How many times has he surprised you? Yet every time he does it, it's still a surprise. Every blessing that comes my way startles me, because it's so far outside the routine of this world.

Are you getting to know the real Jesus? Are you in love with him—or could it be that you are in love with your own image of him? Are you striving to follow the one who created the universe, the one who dwells within your heart, the one who beckons you to come close beside him—or are you merely infatuated with a two-dimensional Sunday school portrait?

Jesus, the lover of your soul, acts outside your expectations. He calls you to listen for his quiet and clear invitations to take risks with him—to live and act and speak and be in ways you may never before have considered. Surprising, unexpected, stretching, and fulfilling ways.

Perhaps your idea to do something extraordinary—that ministry effort you've dismissed as impossible—is really Jesus trying to surprise you. Or the spiritual gift you think you may have but you're a little too afraid to make sure, pooh-poohing it as crazy *(Who am I to think I could do that?)*—maybe that's an outside-the-box experience waiting to happen. Or that major donation you fantasize about making to a ministry organization you greatly respect, but you fear a market reversal—who knows what Jesus could do with that?

What is Jesus calling you to do that has prompted you to say, "You've got to be kidding"?

"Before you dismiss anything as impossible or crazy, come," Jesus says. "Come and see for yourself. Get to know me. See who I really am."

❋ *Jesus, sometimes you make me uncomfortable. I don't know what to expect. I like to keep you in a box so you don't overwhelm me or challenge me or surprise me too much. But I realize that when I do that, I am separated from the real you. I don't want that. I want you. I want to be surprised. I want to be an authentic follower. Help me to expect the unexpected today. Help me to see you in the surprising challenges I face.*

ten

KNOWN, AND LOVED ANYWAY

> When Jesus saw Nathanael coming he said, "There's a real Israelite, not a false bone in his body."
>
> Nathanael said, "Where did you get that idea? You don't know me."
>
> Jesus answered, "One day, long before Philip called you here, I saw you under the fig tree."
>
> Nathanael exclaimed, "Rabbi! You are the Son of God, the King of Israel!"
>
> Jesus said, "You've become a believer simply because I say I saw you one day sitting under the fig tree? You haven't seen anything yet!" (John 1:47–50)

Sometimes I like to read obituaries. In our local newspaper well-written obituaries recount in warm and colorful ways the lives they recall. One recent obituary chronicled the simple life of a never-married woman who was active in her church and garden club and who had built a web of relationships in her community. Everybody knew Vicky. And yet they didn't.

When she died, it became apparent that Vicky was quite a wealthy woman who had generously, and in many cases anonymously, shared her wealth with a number of humanitarian causes, both in the United States and around the world, as well as with several educational institutions, most of which served underprivileged young people. She had given of herself generously and quietly for years. And no one had a clue. The revelation of gracious generosity served as one last surprise gift from her to her many friends.

Most of us invest a lot of time and energy in getting to know the people closest to us, and yet sometimes it seems impossible to know another person fully—to see inside a mind and heart, to grasp someone's motives and dreams. After all, we can only know what another person wants us to know.

We all tend to be self-protective. We want desperately to be known, yet we construct walls around our heart so no one can hurt us in the knowing. So we move through life feeling like orphans, caught in an existential catch-22, seeking to be known but at the same time preventing it.

Nobody really knows us. And there's a big problem with that: Who can truly love us if they don't truly know us?

When a doubtful Nathanael was led to Jesus, the Lord indicated he knew the true Nathanael, the inner person. Nathanael scoffed at this. After all, Jesus had never even met him before. How could this Nazarene know the sort of person he was?

But Nathanael's opinion dramatically changed after Jesus spoke a few words to him. Somehow, sometime earlier, Jesus had seen Nathanael under a fig tree, doing something that revealed his true identity as an authentically good man. Nathanael must have thought his act had gone unnoticed. But he had been seen. And known. And loved. By Jesus.

Just as Jesus saw and knew Nathanael, he sees and knows you. He knows your life, your motives, your personality, and your needs. He knows the good you yearn to do, the private acts of kindness and charity, the dreams that keep you going. He knows the pain that sears your heart, the wants that drive you, the fear that sometimes freezes you into inaction.

Jesus sees you. Knows you. And loves you.

Let this reality seep into your conscious life, perhaps with some sort of visual reminder—a sticky note with your name and Nathanael's written on it, for instance. Let yourself become aware of Jesus' constant, loving gaze toward you.

When you live as one known and loved, then you will open yourself up to all sorts of possibilities, because that realization is just the beginning of a lifetime of authentic love.

Jesus is right. "You haven't seen anything yet!"

❋ *Jesus, I want to be known. I want to be honest with you. I want to tear down the walls around my heart—not only to you, but also to all the other important people in my life. Help me to love and to experience your love. Help me to know and be known.*

eleven

THE REAL YOU

> During the time he was in Jerusalem, those days of the Passover Feast, many people noticed the signs he was displaying and, seeing they pointed straight to God, entrusted their lives to him. But Jesus didn't entrust his life to them. He knew them inside and out, knew how untrustworthy they were. He didn't need any help in seeing right through them.
>
> (John 2:23–25)

All of us have had people in our lives—acquaintances, friends, coworkers, perhaps even a spouse—whom we thought we knew, whom we believed when they told us their feelings and thoughts and life stories. Yet they ultimately revealed themselves to be dishonest and deceptive, causing us to feel used and betrayed by them.

Sometimes we've even realized we've been such a person.

When we learn that someone we know has not been honest with us or routinely spins the truth for personal gain, it is difficult, perhaps even impossible, for the relationship to survive at a very deep level.

In a love relationship such as the one we are pursuing with Jesus and Jesus is pursuing with us, the stakes are even higher. If such a relationship is to grow and thrive, it must be bathed in honesty and openness and vulnerability. Even when we don't come out looking so good. Even when the truth hurts. For without utter honesty, we cannot know Christ's utter love for us. A relationship based on anything less than that depth of honesty is not really a relationship.

This raises some important questions we must ask ourselves:

- Am I truly honest with Jesus?
- Are there aspects of my personality or behavior I'm trying to keep hidden from him, from others, even from myself?
- Do I realize that all the pages of the book of my life are already open to him?
- Am I being honest with myself about all this?

If we are not honest and open with Jesus, we're only kidding ourselves. Barbara Brown Taylor shares this story:

> I remember being at a retreat once where the leader asked us to think of someone who represented Christ in our lives. When it came time to share our answers, one woman stood up and said, "I had to think hard about that one. I kept thinking, Who is it who told me the truth about myself so clearly that I wanted to kill him for it?" According to John, Jesus died because he told the truth to everyone he met. He was the truth, a perfect mirror in which people saw themselves in God's own light.[6]

When Jesus performed miracles, signs, and wonders early in his ministry, people swarmed to him, captivated. They even proclaimed themselves his followers, entrusting their hearts to him. But their faith was shallow; they were all talk and no walk. Their relationship with him was a one-way street. All they wanted to know was, What compelling thought might excite our minds? What miracle might we brag to our friends about? What's in this for me?

Jesus saw right through them, and he can see right through us too.

What does Jesus see when he looks inside your heart? Does he see a divided, untrusting, self-centered soul? Does he see faith as shallow as a warm, murky kiddie pool? Does he see a person who is only seeking relief from life's tedium? Does he see someone playing a game, someone simply going through the motions?

Or does he see a heart that's transparent, authentic, honest, and open to him in every sense? A soul yearning to know him, desperate to be with him, committed to following him wherever he leads?

That is the soul to whom Jesus entrusts his heart.

❋ *Jesus, search my heart. Give me insight into my own motives in wanting to know you and follow you. Strip away from my heart the deception and dishonesty, the need for self-protection, the desire to hide certain parts of my life from you. I want us to entrust our hearts to each other forever.*

twelve

THE MOVING SPIRIT

Jesus said, "You're not listening. Let me say it again. Unless a person submits to this original creation—the 'wind hovering over the water' creation, the invisible moving the visible, a baptism into new life—it's not possible to enter God's kingdom. When you look at a baby, it's just that: a body you can look at and touch. But the person who takes shape within is formed by something you can't see and touch—the Spirit—and becomes a living spirit.

"So don't be so surprised when I tell you that you have to be 'born from above'—out of this world, so to speak. You know well enough how the wind blows this way and that. You hear it rustling through the trees, but you have no idea where it comes from or where it's headed next. That's the way it is with everyone 'born from above' by the wind of God, the Spirit of God." (John 3:5–8)

Nicodemus, a prominent religious leader of the group that would ultimately seek Jesus' death, came to Jesus to talk with him under the secrecy of night's darkness. Nicodemus was curious, intrigued. He wanted to know more about this strange man and his challenging teachings. Some things about this man confused him, and he wanted answers.

But the answers Jesus gave him only evoked within Nicodemus more curiosity, greater bafflement, and a deeper spiritual thirst.

Yet, if we struggle to understand Jesus' words, we discover that his invitation to be "born from above" is the key to the spiritual life, the starting point on the pathway to a life of loving relationship with him forever. According to Jesus, we need to start anew with God, as though we were fresh from the womb. As though we were part of the original creation of God forming the world through the Spirit and the Word.

That same Spirit dwells within you today, even now. Rustling through the leaves and branches and limbs of your soul. Moving you. Filling you. Bringing new surprises and unexpected challenges into your life day by day.

To be in a loving relationship with Jesus means recognizing and living within this Spirit-moving reality. It means being willing to start fresh with him, reborn by the Spirit. Willing to trust your divine Parent to care for you and nurture you as you grow in the faith toward maturity. Willing to be moved along by the Spirit in whatever direction the holy wind blows. Willing to live in the tension of the unknown and the confusing. Willing to grow in curiosity and trust and thirst for more. More of Jesus. More of the Spirit. More life. More love.

It's a lifelong task, a seemingly eternal struggle. But you must begin at the beginning. You must be born from above.

❋ *Jesus, I have many questions, many inaccurate expectations and false understandings about what my relationship with you is all about. Help me to hear your invitation to new birth—and accept it. Help me to be open to the moving of the Spirit within my spirit. Give me a thirst for more.*

thirteen

THE PURE LIGHT OF TRUTH

Jesus said, "Listen carefully. I'm speaking sober truth to you. I speak only of what I know by experience; I give witness only to what I have seen with my own eyes. There is nothing second-hand here, no hearsay. Yet instead of facing the evidence and accepting it, you procrastinate with questions. If I tell you things that are plain as the hand before your face and you don't believe me, what use is there in telling you of things you can't see, the things of God?" (John 3:10–12)

Nicodemus came to Jesus searching, wanting to understand who he was. But he couldn't get his mind around the rabbi's revolutionary spiritual concepts. He couldn't let go of his presuppositions and prejudices, his traditions, his well-worn, routine beliefs about how a relationship with God was supposed to work. He couldn't rise above his questions, his confusions, or his doubts to see the pure light of truth.

There is a lot of Nicodemus in all of us.

The world teaches us to watch out for ourselves, to guard our emotions, to cynically doubt good news. As a result, our minds and hearts have slowly, over time, crusted over with stubborn self-protection, like barnacles on the hull of a fishing boat. So, when Jesus reveals to us something that we struggle to understand, we have trouble accepting it and living within it.

If we are open and willing, if we are conscious of our desperate need for Jesus, then the Spirit of God can crack open those crusty barnacles on our heart. If we are willing, the light of Jesus' love, the clear light of undeniable truth, can get in through those cracks, can soften and warm our hearts, making us pliable and vulnerable so we can see the "things that are plain as the hand before your face" and live the "things you can't see, the things of God."

So, listen to Jesus. Listen carefully for his voice. Trust his love for you. Put aside your fears and doubts in the power of the Spirit, just for a moment or two. Let the Spirit crack open your heart a little bit, and the light of Jesus' love and truth will pour in.

❊ *Jesus, your truth is revolutionary, unexpected, astonishing. Your desire for my heart is overwhelming. I feel almost blinded by the little light you have already shed on my crusty soul—and yet I sense there is only the slightest crack through which you are shining. Break through the hard shell of self-protection that surrounds my heart. Help me to yield completely to your loving truth—and to trust you for whatever happens to me as a result.*

fourteen

A WHOLE AND LASTING LIFE

> Jesus said, "This is how much God loved the world: He gave his Son, his one and only Son. And this is why: so that no one need be destroyed; by believing in him, anyone can have a whole and lasting life. God didn't go to all the trouble of sending his Son merely to point an accusing finger, telling the world how bad it was. He came to help, to put the world right again. Anyone who trusts in him is acquitted; anyone who refuses to trust him has long since been under the death sentence without knowing it. And why? Because of that person's failure to believe in the one-of-a-kind Son of God when introduced to him." (John 3:16–18)

Isn't "a whole and lasting life" what most of us hunger for—a life that is rich and full and meaningful and balanced and loving? A life we've never figured out how to make happen? We've tried so many things: Church. Counseling. Support groups. Study groups. We've searched for it in so many empty places: Relationships. Responsibilities. Successes. Power.

Possessions. Perhaps the next attempt, the next avenue, will take us where we want to go. Or perhaps not.

The true and only way to experience a whole and lasting life, to be "right again," is shockingly simple—just three words: Believe in Jesus.

Believe. In. Jesus.

Too simple? Well, yes and no. If it were so easy, more of us would do it. More of us would trust in God's love enough to accept it. But, too often, we fail to believe in Jesus even when we come face-to-face with him. We see an opportunity to serve him that will cost us some time or money, and we turn away when we realize how that cost might affect our own interests. Or we are given a way to overcome some debilitating emotional pain by reaching out and receiving grace and hope, but we decide we're more comfortable living in the accustomed pain than working to release it. Or we sense a call to something that seems far beyond our capabilities, something that could really make a difference, not only in our life but also in many others' lives, yet we simply can't trust God enough to accept it.

We bump up against those opportunities to believe in Jesus every day. Time and time again, Jesus invites us to trust in him, and he says that when we do, we live. Forever. When we don't, we are already under a death sentence.

Jesus is the way to a full and whole and lasting life, the only true source of authentic and eternal life. So, why is it so hard to accept this as truth? Jesus himself anticipates the question, and explains:

> "This is the crisis we're in: God-light streamed into the world, but men and women everywhere ran for the darkness. They went for the darkness because they were not really interested in pleasing God. Everyone who makes a practice of doing evil, addicted to denial and illusion, hates God-light and won't come near it, fearing a painful exposure. But anyone working and living in truth and reality welcomes God-light so the work can be seen for the God-work it is." (John 3:19–21)

When we are getting to know Jesus, we want to run. We will either run toward him, into the light, or we will run away into the darkness—fearing a painful exposure.

But: "Darkness is an unlit wick; it just needs your touch, Beloved, to become a sacred flame."[7]

The only way to experience the depth of God's love is to run toward him, so don't let your fears keep you away.

❋ *Jesus, you keep telling me you love me. And that you love me so much you came to provide the way for me to live, whole and holy, forever. But I keep fighting you. I keep hiding in the darkness. I keep fearing what you will think of me when you really know me. Yet you keep telling me you do know me, inside and out, and that you have cleansed me from my sin, have shined the light of love on the darkness in my soul. Even so, I keep retreating fearfully from you. This may be simple truth, but it is so difficult to accept. Jesus, today let me work and live in the truth, in the God-light, in love, so you can begin the God-work within my heart that I need so much.*

fifteen

EXTRAVAGANT LOVE

> John answered, "The One that God sent speaks God's words. And don't think he rations out the Spirit in bits and pieces. The Father loves the Son extravagantly. He turned everything over to him so he could give it away—a lavish distribution of gifts. That is why whoever accepts and trusts the Son gets in on everything, life complete and forever!" (John 3:34–35)

Beth had been estranged from her grandmother, who represented to her an old way of life—stifling, constraining. She desperately wanted to be her own person, free and unhindered in her choices. She knew her simple-living grandmother had, out of love and concern for her granddaughter, promised her a modest bequest in her will. But for several years that promise wasn't nearly incentive enough to encourage Beth to rebuild the relationship with her grandmother that she had broken.

Before long, Beth's grandmother fell gravely ill. Out of frustrated guilt, Beth traveled to visit her in the hospital, hoping merely to put in an appearance so as not to totally alienate the rest of her family. But her visit had a profound effect on her. She sensed as never before her grandmother's deep, unshakable love for her—no matter how she lived. She realized that her grandmother was concerned about her well-being. It wasn't that she demanded perfection or a personality transplant to gain her approval; she simply wanted the best for her granddaughter. She wanted her to live a fully realized life, happy and true. This realization didn't come so much through the words they spoke as the look in her grandmother's eyes. And it led to a wonderfully loving reunion of related souls—one that would last beyond Beth's grandmother's death.

The last thing on Beth's mind was her grandmother's last will and testament. In no way did it influence her change of heart; after all, she didn't expect it to amount to much of anything she'd want anyway. Rather, her grandmother's love had broken through. Imagine her surprise at learning that her grandmother's estate was far larger than she had known, and imagine the joy she felt as she was able to honor her grandmother through generous stewardship. One of the many generous things she did with the money she inherited was to help fund the construction of a new Sunday school building at her grandmother's beloved church. Beth said she hoped the young people who would be taught there in the years to come would be able to experience the same merciful love of God that she had received through her grandmother.

Extravagant love. Wasteful. Lavish. Limitless. Forever. Our hearts hunger for it. Jesus offers it to us. He holds it out to us and beckons us to take it, to make it ours.

All it takes is our acceptance and trust in his love, and we get in on everything—"life complete and forever!" It's like an eternal Christmas morning with an endless supply of brightly wrapped packages to open. Or like receiving an unexpected bequest beyond our wildest dreams. Or like winning the lottery, times infinity.

Jesus doesn't hold out to us mere money or possessions; he offers us life everlasting, full and complete, in relationship with the Son of God. He offers acceptance, forgiveness, renewal, love, and life to a limitless degree. Such gifts come from the Father, who possesses all things, who has turned it all over to the Son—just so the Son could give them to us. It's the very nature of God to be liberal with love, mercy, and grace. But we must be ready and willing to receive these gifts.

Jesus woos us time and time again. Do you accept his invitation? As you reflect on this question, listen to the prayer of St. Catherine of Siena, as interpreted by poet Daniel Ladinsky:

> "I won't take no for an answer,"
> God began to say
> to me
> when he opened his arms each night
> wanting us to
> dance.[8]

❋ *Jesus, I am so stubborn. So selfish. So blind. So stupid! Once again today you give me an invitation to incredible, unlimited love and joy. I still can hardly understand it, but you persist. Will I turn my back on you again today? Will I leave your side and wander my own path again? Will I ignore the amazing offer of eternal life you hold out to me? Or will I . . . this day . . . say yes?*

sixteen

WALKING DEAD

> Jesus explained, "It's urgent that you get this right: The time has arrived—I mean right now!—when dead men and women will hear the voice of the Son of God and, hearing, will come alive." (John 5:25)

Thich Nhat Hanh writes, "When we look around, we see many people in whom the Holy Spirit does not appear to dwell. They look dead, as though they were dragging around a corpse, their own body."[9]

Such people go through the motions of life. They sleep, wake up by an alarm clock, get ready for school or work, get stuck in traffic, eat, watch television, and then sleep again. Even though they may make some effort to reach out and relate with others—their family members, coworkers, neighbors, even God—they are still dead. They have not come alive to God's glorious purpose for them. They have deadened themselves to experiencing the powerful Spirit of God in their hearts and lives. They have walled themselves off from the sublime love of their Lord.

You've seen such people walking by you on the street, on the subway, in the elevator. Maybe you've seen them in church or in your own home. Perhaps you've even seen such a person in the mirror.

Jesus says the time has arrived to wake up, come alive, and start experiencing real life. It starts by hearing the voice of the Son of God. The voice of love.

Yes, there will be an ultimate resurrection. Just as Christ was raised from the grave, so too will all who follow him. But that will come at a day and an hour and in a way we do not know.

Jesus says the work of resurrection begins today. Right now. When you are born again, you pass from death to life. When you hear God's voice, you pass from death to life. The miracle of resurrection is already happening inside you. Jesus has made your physical death irrelevant.

Your loving Lord desires that you stop and listen. Listen for his quickening, life-giving voice. He is calling you to life, a life as the beloved of God. A life that will last eternally.

Come alive!

❋ *Jesus, I feel dead in my spirit, in my gut. I am tired of dragging around my own corpse. I pray today that I would hear your voice, that you would wake me up and give me new life, so I can know and experience your love and share it with all around me in your power.*

seventeen
SATISFYING THE HUNGER

Jesus said, "I am the Bread of Life. The person who aligns with me hungers no more and thirsts no more, ever. I have told you this explicitly because even though you have seen me in action, you don't really believe me. Every person the Father gives me eventually comes running to me. And once that person is with me, I hold on and don't let go."

(John 6:35–37)

I was recently talking with a friend who has long seemed unable to find a relationship that works, one that could permanently and maturely fulfill the loneliness that grips his heart. He meets a potential romantic partner, and if they click, he becomes absorbed with her. She is the perfect complement to him; everything she does is just right. If she comes from a different background or culture, he learns everything he can about it. He takes up hobbies she has. He does whatever she wants to do and ignores his own interests and desires.

Essentially, my friend loses himself in order to find the love he is so hungry for. He becomes so stifling, so needy, so pushy that he drives away this "perfect love." Instead of embracing him as he so deeply desires her to, she begins to push him away and finally escapes to freedom from his smothering need. So he is crushed, wounded, and lost—until he finds another woman to pursue, and the cycle starts all over again.

As I talked to my friend about his latest situation, I remembered a passage in *The Inner Voice of Love,* in which Henri Nouwen addresses our need for love, our hunger for relationship:

God does not want your loneliness; God wants to touch you in a way that permanently fills your deepest need. It is important that you dare to stay with your pain and

> allow it to be there. You have to own your loneliness and trust that it will not always be there. The pain you suffer now is meant to put you in touch with the place where you most need healing, your very heart. The person who was able to touch that place has revealed to you your pearl of great price. It is understandable that everything you did, are doing, or plan to do seems completely meaningless compared with that pearl. That pearl is the experience of being fully loved. When you experience deep loneliness, you are willing to give up everything in exchange for healing. But no human being can heal that pain.[10]

Only Jesus offers a love that can totally satisfy such a deep hunger and thirst. His love helps us know and face who we are and then builds within us spiritual empowerment and healing, so we can relate to others in much healthier ways. His love helps us grow up, face ourselves, and open our souls to his radical presence. His love burns away our loneliness, because it is no longer such a terrible problem that we must solve by any means.

But before we can experience the satisfaction he offers, we must trust him with our need for love. We must trust that his love, his presence, his peace will be enough to fulfill us and make us whole, so we don't need to scurry around desperately trying to find whatever it is we think we need.

Choose to love Jesus and stay in his embrace. Believe him when he says that once we are with him, he holds on and doesn't let go. That's what must happen if we are to live loved.

❋ *Jesus, I am hungry for what only you, the Bread of Life, can provide: the unshakable, unbreakable love of my lonely heart. I yearn to believe you have what my soul so desperately craves. So I run to you. Thank you for holding me and never letting me go.*

eighteen

DRAWN TO JESUS

Jesus said, "The Father who sent me is in charge. He draws people to me—that's the only way you'll ever come. Only then do I do my work, putting people together, setting them on their feet, ready for the End. This is what the prophets meant when they wrote, 'And then they will all be personally taught by God.' Anyone who has spent any time at all listening to the Father, really listening and therefore learning, comes to me to be taught personally—to see it with his own eyes, hear it with his own ears, from me, since I have it firsthand from the Father. No one has seen the Father except the One who has his Being alongside the Father—and you can see *me*." (John 6:43–46)

Some years ago I knew a woman who felt a nudge to paint, so she tried it, with rather uninspiring results. She kept at it, reading books, going to museums, learning about painting techniques, and still she couldn't seem to get it. It wasn't flowing. It was barely art.

Then she met an artist—a well-known regional painter whose portraits were highly sought, whose landscapes shimmered with soft reality. The more she learned directly from this artist, the more her own unique work began to take shape. From him she began to understand that painting isn't about technique or style, it is about projecting the essence of who you are onto the canvas and making a deep connection with those who come to appreciate your art.

When it comes to our relationship with Jesus, something similar happens. We can spend all our time reading about Jesus, studying the fine points of theology, and learning about doctrine. Those are good activities. But they may not enable us to know his love. Only spending time personally in the presence of the Lover can do that. Only by acknowledging his reality in our midst, following his ways through his Spirit, and keeping the communication lines open with him continually in prayer can we do that.

We can try to live authentically and serve generously out of our own selves, in our own strength and wisdom. But when we meet the Creator personally, our true gifts are unleashed. Jesus' love transforms us, enabling us to live as he did. He is set loose within us to go to work in our heart and soul. He teaches us personally by taking us under his wing and mentoring us, guiding us, challenging us, and loving us.

That's when he starts putting the shattered pieces of our spirit together again and helps us stand back up on our feet—strong, confident, whole, vibrantly alive. And "ready for the End."

❋ *Jesus, I want to come to you to be taught personally—to see the truth with my own eyes, hear it with my own ears, directly from you. Make me into the person God has created me to be. Set me free to be me. I am your eager student.*

nineteen
ULTIMATE INTIMACY

> Jesus said, "Only insofar as you eat and drink flesh and blood, the flesh and blood of the Son of Man, do you have life within you. The one who brings a hearty appetite to this eating and drinking has eternal life and will be fit and ready for the Final Day. My flesh is real food and my blood is real drink. By eating my flesh and drinking my blood you enter into me and I into you. In the same way that the fully alive Father sent me here and I live because of him, so the one who makes a meal of me lives because of me."
>
> (John 6:53–57)

On the surface, Jesus' words may seem rather gruesome. When he first said them, he was addressing Jews, whose strict code of law forbade any drinking of blood. So why did he invite them to do so? Because "by eating my flesh and drinking my blood you enter into me and I into you." The Eucharist provides us with an unforgettable image of what Jesus deeply desires: to be totally a part of us, intimately integrated with us at the cellular level.

To better understand this, think of the food we eat. It can be healthy, nutritious, and life-giving, or it can be junk, adding calories and fat and useless ingredients the body just sloughs off. When we eat the good stuff, our body maintains its health and vitality. We feel better. We look better. We're healthy. We move more vibrantly through our day. We simply live better.

When we make a meal of Jesus, spiritually recalling his sacrifice through the bread and the wine, he does something similar to our spiritual and emotional self. We become more purposeful, more fulfilled. We can more readily take the risks God calls us to, because we're ready for it. He is with us, totally part of us, intimately present.

Unfortunately, as bad as our physical diet can be at times, our spiritual diet can be just as unhealthy and non-nutritious. We feed on shallow pabulum. Or junk. We avoid the basic parts of a healthy spiritual diet or even starve to death spiritually, not making an effort to eat anything.

We have to remember to make Jesus a constant part of our life—to eat him up in a deeply meaningful, deeply spiritual way. That's why our churches observe the Lord's Supper regularly: to remind us that Jesus wants to be a continually intimate part of our lives—to the very core of our being.

The next time you take communion, and every time you take the bread and the wine, remember how deeply Jesus loves you and wants to be with you and in you. He was willing to give up everything this physical life held for him in order to make that happen.

So, what's on your menu today?

❋ *Jesus, I am humbled to know that you want so deeply to be such an intimate part of my life. I know eating the bread and drinking the wine is just a picture, an image of the reality that you offer—the reality of your living, active presence within me. I want to eat heartily.*

twenty

RESISTING LOVE

> Jesus sensed that his disciples were having a hard time with this and said, "Does this throw you completely? What would happen if you saw the Son of Man ascending to where he came from? The Spirit can make life. Sheer muscle and willpower don't make anything happen. Every word I've spoken to you is a Spirit-word, and so it is life-making. But some of you are resisting, refusing to have any part in this."
>
> (John 6:61–64)

I want to believe in Jesus, to follow him, to know him intimately and fully. I want to listen for his "life-making" words whispered to me by the Spirit. I want to hear them and absorb them into the deepest parts of my being. I want them to transform me and work through me to the world around me. I want all that very much.

But I resist. I wrestle. I struggle. I fight. I doubt. I toss it all out, and then I crawl back on humble knees to receive again. Where does my resistance come from?

Jesus knew that some of his followers would ultimately refuse to have "any part in this." Judas we know. Did some of his other followers also doubt and resist? Do you?

All of us resist him at times. The desires of our heart—created out of need and lack and frustration and failure—sometimes outweigh our trust in Jesus. We think we know what's best for us, and it so often doesn't line up with Christ's call on our lives.

For many years I fought Jesus' call to me in one area of my life. In fact, I usually covered my ears to the divine whispers because what I heard didn't fit my own life construct, my assumptions of God's will for me. But slowly, Jesus' words started getting between the fingers I clenched against my ears. The words came through people I trusted, people I knew to be authentic and whole, people who had heard similar beckonings and had finally yielded to them themselves.

Sometimes the words seem too good to be true; other times, too challenging, too strange, too frightening—so we resist. We fight. But when we do, we realize we can't make anything happen in our own power. Only the Spirit can make things happen. Only the Spirit can make life.

Jesus is whispering Spirit-words, life-making words, to you right now. He is calling you to something new, something unexpected, something that may not make complete sense right now.

Do you sense some resistance? That's a good sign. It means you are hearing him. It means you can choose to listen to him—and respond in faith.

❋ *Jesus, I sense a constant inner struggle between my will and yours. Open my ears to your Spirit-words. Open my heart to your loving pull on my will. Melt my resistance. And make life happen in me.*

twenty-one

SPIRITUAL DROUGHT

On the final and climactic day of the Feast, Jesus took his stand. He cried out, "If anyone thirsts, let him come to me and drink. Rivers of living water will brim and spill out of the depths of anyone who believes in me this way, just as the Scripture says." (John 7:37–38)

Some time ago our area experienced a severe drought lasting a number of years. Our lakes were low, with naked, cracked-mud shorelines and waterfalls dripping rather than roaring through lush, green forests. During the early stages of this drought we took our young children whitewater rafting in North Georgia. "We're the adventure family!" I shouted with slightly manufactured excitement and anticipation. I told our kids how much fun we would have moving along in the water, twirling around, rushing through the forest.

We climbed into a huge truck-tire inner tube we had rented. A square sheet of plywood was lashed to the bottom, providing a place to sit, and off we went into the rocky river. Unfortunately, the level of the river was so low there wasn't any "white" to the whitewater. In fact, we'd simply float a few feet and then I would have to climb out to pull the rest of my family in this heavy inner tube across the exposed rocks. When I'd pull it, straining hard over the difficult spots, the plywood board would slide into my shins time and again.

I kept telling the kids, "Surely just ahead the water will be deeper and we'll have great fun then!" But we never did find enough water to move us.

Sometimes that's how my heart feels. The spiritual water level is low. The "rivers of living water" have slowed to a trickle. It's tough going, and I only end up bruised and disappointed. Where is the rush? Where is the spiritual whitewater?

Oh, how we yearn for those rivers of the Spirit to rush through us and spill out of us like a geyser of exuberant love. We read Jesus' words and think, *Hey, why don't I experience this? Why isn't this a constant sensation of my spiritual life?* After all, we believe in Jesus, and this is the work of the Spirit he promised to all who believe.

Perhaps there's a cause-and-effect relationship here that we're not seeing. If we don't sense the rivers of living water pulsing, rushing, flowing through us out of the depths of our being, maybe we're missing something.

It's right here: "If anyone thirsts . . . ."

Throughout John's gospel, Jesus continually reminds us that in order to know his love we have to want it. We have to yearn for it. We have to desire it like a person wandering lost in a hot, dry desert yearns for water. And we have to "come... and drink." Deep, pure refreshment is there, waiting for us, offered to us by our loving Lord. All we need to do is come to him and drink him in. Drink up his presence, his power, his love, his joy. That means giving ourselves some time and a quiet place, letting our mind and heart meditate and pray, opening ourselves to his work within us.

When we do, the rivers of the Spirit will roll and rush and brim and spill out of our depths.

How strong is your thirst right now?

✻ *Jesus, I am thirsty. Maybe I hesitate to come to you and drink. The whitewater of the Spirit can be a little scary, daunting. But it's an adventure of a lifetime. It's the adventure you call me to. So, let me drink up and know you fully.*

twenty-two

BEYOND THE HORIZONS

> Jesus said, "You're tied down to the mundane; I'm in touch with what is beyond your horizons. You live in terms of what you see and touch. I'm living on other terms. I told you that you were missing God in all this. You're at a dead end. If you won't believe I am who I say I am, you're at the dead end of sins. You're missing God in your lives." (John 8:23–24)

Jesus' indictment of the religious leaders of his day reveals the tragedy of a life lived inside the box of faithlessness, a life lived without knowing and experiencing the love of God. These leaders were prominent, successful, and revered by many. They had their lives figured out to the last jot and tittle. They knew exactly what was right and wrong, and they were always right. They certainly weren't shy about telling other people how to live. But Jesus says they were "tied down to the mundane." They lived a life that was shut down. Boxed in. They lived only in this physical world; their souls did not soar into the spiritual realm. Though they thought they represented God in everything they did, Jesus told them they were missing God totally. They were at a dead end, and they did not even know it.

What a tragedy. And how little things change. And yet... when we examine our own hearts, our own motives, our own faith, can we see that we are missing something too? Are we so tied down to the mundane that we can't even look to the horizon of possibility? Are we so caught up in our needs and desires that we're missing God in our lives? Are we so confident that we're right that we deny the rights of other people who are different? Are we living a life without fully knowing Christ's love?

Are we too at a dead end?

I have a friend who has just conquered one of life's dead ends. She decided after years in a secure position to uproot herself, move halfway across the country, and begin again in a challenging position in a religious organization. The new job would stretch her in every way: she had to leave dear friends and family, find a new place to live, learn how to negotiate a brand-new city, even buy a car. She would have to learn new skills and become an expert in challenging endeavors. But she sensed God's call, God's challenge. She was feeling boxed in where she was, seemingly spinning her wheels, and was ready to accept a new challenge.

Has she doubted her decision? Absolutely! Several times, in fact, in the months after her move. But deep down, she knows this is God's challenge for her now and that her loving Lord will see her through it. Some months after she'd moved I called her on the phone to see if she still thought that. But before I could even ask, she said, "I had the most amazing day yesterday. I can't tell you how blessed I was all day. It was one of those days that God was saying, 'See? I told you this was the right decision.'"

Jesus is in touch with what is beyond our horizons. He is already there waiting for us. He is inviting us to live on other terms—his.

The religious leaders took offense at Jesus' indictment and continued to live inside their boxes of false certainty. We, however, have the opportunity to go with our Lord beyond the horizons of everything we ever thought possible in life—and, by doing so, gain a new understanding and experience of his love for us.

That's not a dead end. It's the start of a new life.

❋ *Jesus, you challenge me to let go of my preconceptions and question my easy answers. You lovingly beckon me to a new place, way outside my comfort zone. You are already there, waiting for me. Here I come.*

twenty-three
CRAZY LOVE

> Jesus said, "I'm not crazy. I simply honor my Father, while you dishonor me. I am not trying to get anything for myself. God intends something gloriously grand here and is making the decisions that will bring it about. I say this with absolute confidence. If you practice what I'm telling you, you'll never have to look death in the face." (John 8:49–51)

Lately, a friend of mine has been experiencing the delight and excitement of falling in love. He is absolutely infatuated with a woman, and she with him. He tries to spend as much time as he can with his girlfriend, taking long lunches from work, spending as many evenings with her as he can, taking trips with her, talking with her on the phone, emailing her, even instant-messaging her online during the day. When he's not with her or talking with her, he's telling other people about her and showing them pictures of her on his cell phone.

He is love-dumb. Crazy in love!

They've been seeing each other for more than three months as I write this, but he seems to be only getting crazier. Surely they'll start acting like adults again. Surely this craziness will cool off and they will move into more mature love (oh, by the way, my friend is in his late forties). He told me the other day he kept waiting for that to happen, but he only seems to love her more deeply each day.

What if we could experience God's love with that much intensity, that much closeness, that much delight?

Love can make you crazy. The world can look at a man or a woman who is deeply in love and shake its head in amazement. Love can even make some people angry because they aren't experiencing head-over-heels love themselves.

Something like that happened to Jesus. He was so deeply in love with the Father, and the Father with him, that the religious leaders thought he was crazy, demon-possessed even. Jesus kept telling them how much the Father loved them, and he backed up his incredible claims and his amazing miracles with the explanation that he was only doing what the Father sent him to do. They didn't like that idea, because Jesus' words and actions did not fit into their convenient, self-protective understanding of what God should be saying and doing.

This divine love relationship may have been extravagant, and it may not have made much sense to human minds. But it wasn't infatuation. It wasn't frivolous in the least. It was essential. It was defining. This love relationship with the Father made Jesus who he was and compelled him to do what he did. Jesus confronted humanity with all the love and truth of God, right there in the flesh. Where there was pain and grief, he brought healing and hope. Where there was emptiness and loneliness, he brought fullness and community. Where there was injustice and antagonism, he brought truth and peace.

Jesus offers this kind of defining love to those who come to him, who struggle to know him, who enter into his way of life, who choose to receive his love. This may seem crazy to people who really don't know him or don't understand what God is all about. But it can bring us to the place where life finally makes some sense, as crazy as it may seem.

Recently I came across a passage in an article that speaks of this Father/Son relationship:

> The Son's love for his Father is all consuming. . . . John tells us that the manifestation of the love union between

> the Father and the Son . . . extends to include the disciples who have come to believe in the identity of the Son as the one sent by the Father. . . . The disciples' identity, individuality, and significance are found in the love union shared by the Father and the Son. The disciples are in some sense an extension of the divine love union. . . . The love that is shared by the Father and the Son is the same love that is shared among the disciples.[11]

That is revolutionary love. Essential love. Defining love. And yes, crazy love. It is offered to all who know Jesus, who live in his love, who follow his way, who "practice what I'm telling you."

❋ *Jesus, I love you, and I sense your love for me. Yet I sometimes feel I don't have the first clue about what that love is, how it works, what I'm supposed to do with it. Show me the way. Show me how to live in constant mutual love with you, just as you do with the Father. Thank you for loving me.*

twenty-four

RECOGNIZING HIS VOICE

> Jesus heard that they had thrown him out, and went and found him. He asked him, "Do you believe in the Son of Man?"
>
> The man said, "Point him out to me, sir, so that I can believe in him."
>
> Jesus said, "You're looking right at him. Don't you recognize my voice?"
>
> "Master, I believe," the man said, and worshiped him.
>
> (John 9:35–38)

Sometimes I am glad I have a phone with the caller ID feature. If I know a sales call is coming in, I can ignore it. When a friend or family member calls, I can answer the phone readily. Yet caller ID takes some of the fun and mystery out of answering the phone. I no longer have the experience of picking up the phone, answering with a questioning "Hello?" and then hearing a voice I haven't heard in a while—an old friend calling to catch up, someone in my family with unexpected good news, or a grandchild just wanting to say, "I love you." I hear that voice and, even before I hear a name, I already know who it is. And I'm ready to listen.

So, what if Jesus called you up? Would he sound familiar to you?

In the passage above, Jesus had healed a man born blind on the Sabbath. In an effort to pin a serious charge on this trouble-making rabbi, the religious leaders had interrogated the blind man who now could see. He spoke earnestly on behalf of his healer and was promptly thrown out in the street.

Jesus sought him out. At first the man didn't recognize Jesus—after all, he had been blind. But then he recognized Jesus' voice. And he believed. And then he worshiped.

We too can be so spiritually blind that we fail to recognize the presence of Jesus. We look right at him and don't see him. We hear his voice in the depths of our soul, but we don't recognize it as his.

Maybe you've experienced this. You know the times when you've struggle over a situation in life, trying to make a wise, godly decision about it. It feels as though you are burning up thousands of brain cells trying to figure it all out. You know that whatever you decide could affect other people's lives. You talk at length to several people you trust. You do a lot of reading about some of the issues involved. You ponder and think and question and probe.

And then the answer just kind of clicks. The "simple" and right solution comes into focus. You realize that Jesus has been speaking to you for some time about this. You hadn't been able to hear him before because you were so busy trying to figure it out yourself.

This happens to me often, it seems, with issues large and small. One recent weekend I worked over in my head a recommendation my boss made to me on that Friday about taking on a new responsibility in our media organization. My immediate reaction was to pooh-pooh it. But he urged me to think and pray about it over the weekend. It made so much sense and solved a lot of problems, but it also would put me in a new role with much more risk and responsibility. Did I want that? Was I ready for that? What if I failed? What if I hurt the ministry? What if this "solution" only caused more problems—for me or the organization? As I bounced the idea off a couple of friends, they acted as though this decision were a no-brainer. And yet I still didn't decide for sure until later the next week. Deep down I knew what to do and I was simply fighting it—until I reached a point of surrender to the whispered invitation of the Spirit to go for it.

Jesus is with us, speaking to us all along. When we recognize his voice, we sense an incredible, healing, loving peace. Later in John's gospel he explains further:

> "If a person climbs over or through the fence of a sheep pen instead of going through the gate, you know he's up to no good—a sheep rustler! The shepherd walks right up to the gate. The gatekeeper opens the gate to him and the sheep recognize his voice. He calls his own sheep by name and leads them out. When he gets them all out, he leads them and they follow because they are familiar with his voice. They won't follow a stranger's voice but will scatter because they aren't used to the sound of it." (John 10:1–5)

Do you hear Jesus' voice? He is calling you by name. He is beckoning you to follow him. He is leading you out of the fenced-in pen of your life. You do not know where he is taking you. But you know his voice, and you trust him.

So, answer him. "Master, I believe."

❋ *Jesus, here you are, standing right in front of me, and I don't see you. Speak to me. I do recognize your voice. I hear what you are saying. And I believe. Thank you for your loving, healing touch today.*

twenty-five

PROTECTED FOR GOOD

> Jesus answered, "I give my sheep real and eternal life. They are protected from the Destroyer for good. No one can steal them from out of my hand. The Father who put them under my care is so much greater than the Destroyer and Thief. No one could ever get them away from him." (John 10:28–29)

A couple of months ago I ran into a friend who was obviously upset about something. He and his wife had been trying to cope with their grown son's problems with addiction to drugs and alcohol, as well as with an overall depression and frustration with the challenges of his life and marriage and fatherhood. Some months earlier, their son had seemed to be making some progress—working on his problems in therapy, seeking support of healthy friends, getting the medical help he needed, and starting to attend a church after several years away. He had earlier left his wife, but she had taken him back and they were working on their marriage.

But after months of this slow but steady progress, once again he dropped out. He didn't come home after work and didn't call. He was gone for several days with no word to anyone. He had relapsed and run away. His wife and his parents were deeply concerned and frustrated. Yet my friend said he somehow knew his son was alive and safe—somewhere.

We prayed together for his son's safety and God's care. More recently I learned the son did call the following day and explained his plight. He was filled with remorse and apologies, and realized he needed more help. Before long he went back home. But he couldn't face the major steps he needed to take to overcome his addiction problems, and a few weeks later he was gone again. This time my friend wasn't so sure what would happen.

We often hear stories like this. People get sucked into the ways that lead to destruction, to the theft of true life. But in those cases, can we believe Jesus' promises that those who are in his loving arms are safe from the hands of the Destroyer? That they cannot be stolen, ripped out of Jesus' arms? That they are under his care, no matter what? That they cannot be lost? We hope so. We pray so. Many similar stories have happy endings. But far too many others end in inexplicable tragedy.

We may never understand some of life's more devastating whys. All we can do is trust that Jesus is there and that somehow he means what he says. Even when the situation looks bleak and overwhelming, we need to hear our loving Shepherd's assurance of eternal care. And rest in it.

Our definition of what that means, frankly, may be different from what God has in mind. As I write this, my friend's situation is unresolved. His son is still out there somewhere. He and his family and circle of support have a long road ahead of them. Perhaps the son will be reunited once again, for good. Or the same behavior pattern may be repeated numerous times. No one knows yet.

But even so, through it all God showers our lives with grace. Even when we stray, even when we go into self-destruct mode, we are still in Jesus' hands. He will be there, ready to comfort and help when we are ready to go to him and throw ourselves into his loving arms.

❋ *Jesus, sometimes I really need to know and trust that I am yours forever. Even when I jump out of your arms and live life my way, you are ready to gather me back into your loving embrace. Keep me safe and secure from the world's attacks and immune to the threats of the Destroyer.*

twenty-six
A HUMBLE CLEANSING

So he got up from the supper table, set aside his robe, and put on an apron. Then he poured water into a basin and began to wash the feet of the disciples, drying them with his apron. When he got to Simon Peter, Peter said, "Master, *you* wash *my* feet?"

Jesus answered, "You don't understand now what I'm doing, but it will be clear enough to you later."

Peter persisted, "You're not going to wash my feet—ever!"

Jesus said, "If I don't wash you, you can't be part of what I'm doing."

"Master!" said Peter. "Not only my feet, then. Wash my hands! Wash my head!" (John 13:4–9)

Have you ever been to a foot-washing service? They make me a little uncomfortable. A church I attended for many years had one after a Passover meal every Maundy Thursday, recreating the Last Supper the disciples shared with Jesus. I always made sure my toenails were trimmed, my feet clean. Sometimes I put lotion on them beforehand, so whoever ended up washing my feet wouldn't notice the dry, tough skin on my soles.

It's such a simple act, yet I am strangely moved every time I let myself experience it. To wash someone else's dirty feet requires some measure of humility, sacrifice, and love. So does allowing another person to wash your feet.

Foot-washing ceremonies make me glad the church adopted the Eucharist—communion with bread and wine—as the primary sacrament, rather than foot-washing. Only John's gospel includes this account of what happened during the Last Supper and ignores the bread and wine, the body and blood. I've always wondered why. Then I think of the love John had for his Master and John's desire to capture this intimate snapshot of the intense, servant-hearted love Jesus had for all his companions.

Jesus knew where he was heading—the cross. He knew what would happen to him—a painful death. And he knew why he would sacrifice himself—for love.

But in the meantime, Jesus offered another glimpse of the love God has for us by washing each disciple's feet. As he and his companions gathered for their last meal together, Jesus saw that no one had taken care of this humble task of hospitality: washing the dirty, dusty feet of those who had come to dine. While this was normally the nasty, even humiliating task of a lowly servant—someone the recipients would hardly notice under ordinary circumstances—Jesus took it upon himself to perform it. He stripped nearly naked, kneeled down before each one, took their dusty feet in his hands, and washed them.

Yes, Jesus did it! Why? Peter was incredulous and probably more than a little embarrassed for his Master. As usual, Peter didn't understand. Then the truth started to sink into his brain. Jesus had to cleanse him if he was to be part of Jesus' family, his movement, his circle of love, his work in the world. Once Peter understood this, he didn't want Jesus to stop with his feet. He wanted the works.

Peter's filthy feet were washed and cleaned. So was his heart.

The other day I was talking with a pastor who mentioned that his church service the next Sunday was going to be a little unusual: it would incorporate a marriage ceremony. The couple had, interestingly enough, met months earlier at the foot-washing service in that same sanctuary during Holy Week. Their lives had been brought together by this sacrament of loving service, and they would be joined together in the sacrament of matrimony to love and serve not only each other but also the world around them. What a beautiful picture of the loving relationship Jesus calls us to, with him.

Jesus does the same thing today with us as he did with Peter in the upper room—he washes us, makes us clean and new, makes us "part of what I'm doing."

But we, like Peter, have to let him.

❋ *Jesus, you offer us such beautiful examples of loving service, of humility and care. I feel the need to be washed by you today, and I accept it humbly. Keep your sacrificial service in my mind today, so I can be alert to ways I can lovingly serve others—even if it feels uncomfortable.*

twenty-seven

THE ROAD TO LOVE

> Jesus said, "I am the Road, also the Truth, also the Life. No one gets to the Father apart from me. If you really knew me, you would know my Father as well. From now on, you do know him. You've even seen him!" (John 14:6–7)

Jesus prepares his beloved followers for what lies ahead. He says, "You already know the road I'm taking" (14:4). The disciples may have known, but they didn't want to believe it. He had given them many hints along the way, but now he was telling them point blank: He was going to die. The road he walked led to a cross.

Of course, as you might expect, they still didn't quite grasp the import of Jesus' words. In fact, Thomas, the one who would come to be known as the Doubter, interrupted him: "Master, we have no idea where you're going. How do you expect us to know the road?" (14:5).

Even knowing the end of the story, I certainly identify with Thomas at times.

It's so easy for some Christians to insist they know the absolute truth and that their way is the only road that really leads to God. But Jesus wasn't saying that holding the correct doctrines, believing the right theology, is the way to God. He was saying *he* is the way to God. There is no road to follow: he is the road. His life is the way.

The Jesus who can take us to the Father is the one who lived and walked and ministered and healed and wept and taught and loved. His is the way of simplicity, humility, peace, honesty, compassion, service, sacrifice, and, above all, love. His life and teachings don't just shine the way on the road to God; they *are* the road to God.

You've been working diligently to get to know Jesus personally, to fully understand and accept his love. But are you on the right road? Where does it really lead? Jesus says something like this: "If you know me then you know the Father. You know who God is and what God desires of his children. And you know what road to travel, what truth to hold on to, what life to live."

Jesus is the road. He is the truth. He is the life. Follow his way—follow him—and he will take you straight to the Father's heart, the place where you can live loved.

❋ *Jesus, I seem to be taking a lot of wrong turns, finding myself lost in the woods of my desires. In your presence, I am on the road to God. Help me to focus on you, knowing that by doing so I'll get exactly where I want to go.*

twenty-eight

DIRECT ACCESS

Jesus said, "This is what I want you to do: Ask the Father for whatever is in keeping with the things I've revealed to you. Ask in my name, according to my will, and he'll most certainly give it to you. Your joy will be a river overflowing its banks!

"I've used figures of speech in telling you these things. Soon I'll drop the figures and tell you about the Father in plain language. Then you can make your requests directly to him in relation to this life I've revealed to you. I won't continue making requests of the Father on your behalf. I won't need to. Because you've gone out on a limb, committed yourselves to love and trust in me, believing I came directly from the Father, the Father loves you directly."

(John 16:23–27)

Often when we are trying to reach a prominent business or religious leader by telephone, we have to go through a number of assistants, all of whom are doing their best to protect their boss from the swarm of people who want something from him or her. Though understandable, it can be quite frustrating. The receptionist passes us on to the administrative assistant, who gives us to the personal assistant, who gives us to the receptionist again. And that's if you're lucky enough to get a human being on the line.

Some years ago I dialed the phone number of someone I thought I would never be able to reach directly. He was a major national figure in the church. I'd found the number on a website, hoping against hope to get a message to him, but was sure I'd have to run through the gauntlet of associates and assistants and probably get lost in a voicemail maze. Imagine my astonishment when this well-known person picked the phone up on the second ring. He was quite accessible, in every sense.

So is God. We have direct access to the God of the universe, who wants us to know and understand that truth. We have the privilege of speaking directly to God, and we can ask whatever we will. Imagine that. Direct access to the one who has promised to love you. Completely. Perfectly. Unconditionally. Forever. It's only possible because you have chosen to receive God's love, because you've "gone out on a limb, committed yourselves to love and trust in me."

So, go ahead. Ask for whatever you want. God promises that if you are living in the Spirit of Jesus, marked inside and out by his compassionate truth, then "he'll most certainly give it to you." Is it any wonder Jesus says, "Your joy will be a river overflowing its banks"?

❋ *Jesus, thanks to you I can enter the presence of the Father, speak directly to the God of the universe. I am honored to be heard, to be known and loved and enjoyed. Thank you for opening the way for me.*

twenty-nine

RIGHT WHERE HE IS

Jesus said, "Father, I want those you gave me
To be with me, right where I am,
So they can see my glory, the splendor you gave me,
Having loved me
Long before there ever was a world.
Righteous Father, the world has never known you,
But I have known you, and these disciples know
That you sent me on this mission.
I have made your very being known to them—
Who you are and what you do—
And continue to make it known,
So that your love for me
Might be in them
Exactly as I am in them." (John 17:24–26)

Jesus prayed that those whom the Father gave him—including you—would be right where he is, right with him, intimately connected. Your head on his chest in the upper room, hearing his heartbeat, feeling the warmth of his life.

Henri Nouwen wrote a passage in his book *The Inner Voice of Love* that I find almost excruciating in its longing for this kind of experience of love—excruciating because I too have felt the same longing:

> You are looking for ways to meet Jesus. You are trying to meet him not only in your mind but also in your body. You seek his affection, and you know that this affection involves his body as well as yours. He became flesh for you so that you could encounter him in the flesh and receive his love in the flesh. But something remains in you that prevents this meeting. There is still a lot of shame and guilt stuck away in your body, blocking the

> presence of Jesus. . . . You will not be able to meet Jesus in your body while your body remains full of doubts and fears. Jesus came to free you from these bonds and to create in you a space where you can be with him. . . . You cannot make yourself different. Jesus came to give you a new heart, a new spirit, a new mind, and a new body. Let him transform you by his love and so enable you to receive his affection in your whole being.[12]

Jesus is so full of love for you that he yearns to be present with you, fully and intimately. He is working on your heart and your spirit and your mind in order to make it so.

Do you know this yet? Is it dawning on your soul? Do you sense him at work? Are you cooperating with him, working to tear down the walls of fear and doubt that keep him out? Are you opening yourself up to him, exactly as you are? Have you made the decision to stop pretending and hiding and protecting yourself for fear he will discover who you really are?

He already knows. And he still loves you. So, let him do his work of transformation. He can't wait to get started.

❋ *Jesus, this is scary. The more I know about your love, the more I want it—but I still fear it. I acknowledge my self-protection, and I also acknowledge my utter need for your loving presence. Thank you for letting me be with you, right where you are. Do your work on my heart.*

thirty

THE WINE OF LOVE

> Jesus, seeing that everything had been completed so that the Scripture record might also be complete, then said, "I'm thirsty."
>
> A jug of sour wine was standing by. Someone put a sponge soaked with the wine on a javelin and lifted it to his mouth.

After he took the wine, Jesus said, "It's done . . . complete." Bowing his head, he offered up his spirit. (John 19:28–30)

Jesus' ministry was launched with the supernatural creation of wine at a merry celebration. It was the very best wine, which he had miraculously fashioned from water, served to the surprised guests at a wedding in Cana. *This was the wine of life.*

His ministry ends with wine in a much crueler, darker setting. Cheap, sour wine forced into his parched, dry mouth by a sponge at the end of a Roman spear. *This was the wine of death.*

We remember Christ's life and his death with the wine of the Eucharist, representing his blood shed on the cross. Remembering him, honoring his deep, sacrificial love for us every time we drink it. *This is the wine of love.*

We thirst for that love. Our souls are parched and dry for it. Jesus willingly gives it—abundantly, fully, beyond our possibility even to endure it.

Look what he did to love you.

❋ *Jesus, your sacrifice for me takes my breath away. I know you love me. I thirst for you and for your love. Help me to die to my own selfish, self-protective, deceptive ways and to live in your love. And to give that love away in sacrificial ways.*

Part Two

EXPERIENCING HIS LOVE

thirty-one
A GENEROUS BOUNTY

We all live off his generous bounty,
  gift after gift after gift.
We got the basics from Moses,
  and then this exuberant giving and receiving,
This endless knowing and understanding—
  all this came through Jesus, the Messiah. (John 1:16–17)

A friend once recounted to me in passionate tones a special church retreat he had participated in. He had been going through a rough time personally, feeling as though he had hit a brick wall with his relationships, his career, and his faith. So, with the encouragement of some friends, he had signed up for the weekend in the hope that God would meet him there.

That proved to be an understatement. Unknown to my friend, the leaders of the retreat had contacted dozens of his friends and family members beforehand, asking them to write him a loving, supportive letter. At the retreat, one of the leaders read the letters out loud to him. As letter after letter of affirmation and encouragement was read, my friend broke down repeatedly, overwhelmed by the cleansing, abounding love of so many people. He was embraced and nurtured continually. He told me it felt as though Jesus himself had given him a big hug all weekend long.

During that weekend, he experienced loving care as he never had before, which shook him out of his doldrums and gave him renewed purpose in life. For days afterward he glowed with the loving affirmation of so many people.

But before long, all that affirmation and love began to dissipate. The warm feelings subsided. Real life set in. The weekend became a pleasant memory—never to be forgotten, assuredly, but certainly what he had experienced that one weekend bore no resemblance to his everyday life. He realized that he had to find true meaning in life from a mature, continual relationship with Jesus, not just from powerful weekend retreats.

What if we could live in such a way as to experience constantly the fullness of God's love, to be overwhelmed continually by love and encouragement and support? Would it be too much to bear? Would it dissipate and become less meaningful? Or would it invigorate and energize us to live far beyond our puny expectations, to stop searching for love and fulfillment in this world and find it in Jesus, so we can really make a difference in this needy world?

According to John, Jesus wants to share "his generous bounty" with each of us. He desires to give us gift after gift of love and care and insight and challenge. What keeps us from truly experiencing that? Perhaps the key is right before us: his bounty is an "exuberant giving and receiving" of holy love. It's not just unidirectional. It calls us to give and serve in love, so we may in turn receive love. Endlessly.

❋ *Jesus, this seems too good to be true. Is it? Help me to trust you enough to find out, to see the possibilities, to begin to both give and receive the gifts and experience the love you want to lavish upon all of us.*

thirty-two

MERE MIRACLES

When the host tasted the water that had become wine (he didn't know what had just happened but the servants, of course, knew), he called out to the bridegroom, "Everybody I know begins with their finest wines and after the guests have had their fill brings in the cheap stuff. But you've saved the best till now!"

This act in Cana of Galilee was the first sign Jesus gave, the first glimpse of his glory. And his disciples believed in him.

(John 2:9–11)

It was as if Jesus couldn't help himself. He didn't think it was time to reveal who he was; he even had some words with his mother about it. But before anyone knew it, he had accomplished his first miracle, the "first glimpse of his glory." Then the party really got going.

It often requires ready eyes and a prepared heart to see such glimpses of Jesus at work in our lives, loving us, challenging us, preparing us for more. We must be intentional about this if we want to recognize Jesus' miracles in the midst of life's tedious monotony or its painful difficulties.

What glorious miracles will you glimpse today?

- a beautiful sunrise washing over the cold, dark earth with a cleansing flood of warm, bright light.
- a child's uninhibited laughter and dancing eyes.
- a friend's strong embrace and word of encouragement.
- safe passage through a difficult storm.
- a surprisingly satisfying answer to a vexing question.
- a realization of an important step to take in life.
- an unexpected provision of a resource you've been lacking.
- good news about a family member's long illness.
- an unexpected celebration.
- a meaningful worship service.
- a cleansing time of prayer.
- a phone call from a loved one.
- a good book.
- clarity regarding a calling you've been wrestling with.
- a deeply satisfying, rejuvenating night's sleep.
- a feeling of settled trust that God is in control and all will be well.
- a realization that you have let go of your anxiety over someone close to you, putting that person in God's hands.

Maybe, like me, you have to force yourself to open your eyes and see such things as glimpses of Jesus' glory. For instance, it's easy for me to think back over the past few days and see the mountain of work I've had to tackle for my job, my duties to loved ones, and my responsibilities to pay my bills, revise my manuscript, deal with unexpected situations. On the surface, it hasn't been much fun. Then I stop and think about the glimpses: the smile from someone who loves me. The phone call from a dear friend thinking about me. The incredibly gorgeous, crisp, fall weather. A wonderful meal shared with friends. On and on the glimpses come to me. If I can see them for what they are, they can change my whole outlook.

Jesus "saved the best till now!" Right now. Always *now.* But we have to recognize his loving hand at work and open ourselves to experience it.

❋ *Jesus, I do believe. I see you at work in myriad ways in my life and in the world around me. Help me to recognize your hand in all the miracles of life—major and minor—and give you the praise and devotion you deserve.*

thirty-three

OPEN CHANNELS

> Jesus put together a whip out of strips of leather and chased them out of the Temple, stampeding the sheep and cattle, upending the tables of the loan sharks, spilling coins left and right. He told the dove merchants, "Get your things out of here! Stop turning my Father's house into a shopping mall!" That's when his disciples remembered the Scripture, "Zeal for your house consumes me." (John 2:15–17)

At first glance Jesus' shocking actions in the temple hardly seem loving. Yet they reveal his inexhaustible passion for his Father, a passion and zeal that drives all his actions. The Father yearns to be with his children; he seeks our company and desires that we approach him in right ways.

Jesus knew that. He also knew the ways of the temple merchants actually hindered rather than helped people worship God. God seeks a clean, pure, authentic connection with us, an open channel of relationship. But we tend to clog that connection with human-concocted rules and regulations. We get so focused on the way we approach God that we neglect to actually do the approaching.

In this case, Jesus forcefully cleans out the garbage that chokes the channel of relationship with God. This cleansing is an act of love because its purpose is to restore the direct connection between God and God's people.

What would Jesus find in your temple—your life, your body, your mind? Would he find something that needed to be cleaned out, overturned, and chased off before you could enjoy a connection with him?

Perhaps shame hinders you from coming to God, or irrational expectations of what should and shouldn't happen when you fall into Jesus' embrace. Or maybe busy habits or harmful behaviors distract you from the true way. Perhaps it's a shattered dream or a broken heart, or a confused mind or a hectic schedule. Or it may be a simple misunderstanding of how one can approach God in faith.

Experiencing Jesus' cleansing may be painful in the moment, but it is ultimately a loving act. Because it sets things right, it reopens the way to God by cleaning out the garbage in our soul. Jesus is zealous for you, consumed by love for you. He wants you wholly. And holy.

✻ *Jesus, prepare my heart for your zealous cleansing. Knock over the tables of wrong thinking and selfish purpose. Chase out the fears and the shame and the delusions that keep my focus away from you. Fill my temple with your loving presence.*

thirty-four

RUNNING TO JESUS

Jesus said, "In the same way that Moses lifted the serpent in the desert so people could have something to see and then believe, it is necessary for the Son of Man to be lifted up—and everyone who looks up to him, trusting and expectant, will gain a real life, eternal life." (John 3:14–15)

There's very little to compare to the feeling of being welcomed by a toddler grandchild. Usually, as soon as Tyler sees me walk through the door, he jumps up and runs to me with his arms outstretched, giddily yelling, "Bagah! Bagah!" (which loosely translated means "Grandpa"). My heart overflows with love for him, and I scoop him into my arms and hug and kiss him, and he returns the hugs, laughing and joyful.

When it comes to my approaching Jesus, I want to be like Tyler. I want to run to Jesus without hesitation and jump into his arms, "trusting and expectant." And that's what Jesus wants me to do. That's what relationship with Jesus is supposed to look like.

But there are other times Tyler would just as soon run away from me, avoid me, or whine at me. He'd much rather furiously play than take his afternoon nap. He'd much rather eat sugary snacks than vegetables. He'd much rather play outside for yet another hour than come inside for the rest he and his grandpa need. Those times when he pushes me away can hurt. When he ignores my requests or whines or boldly refuses to obey, I want to say, "Don't you know I'm doing this because I love you and I want the best for you?"

How often must Jesus want to say that to me! Thankfully, no matter how much I ignore Jesus or turn away from him, he still loves me—even more than I love Tyler, no matter what he does.

What holds us back from approaching Jesus exuberantly, like a joyful child, fully trusting, totally consumed with his presence? For one thing, we're adults, not three-year-olds. We're sophisticated! And we really don't need anyone else, do we? We've learned pretty much how to get through life with our own wits, on our own strength. Besides, we have been hurt too many times already when we've let our hearts be so vulnerable to someone else. Why risk that hurt again?

And what happens after we run into his embrace? What will he want us to do? How will he want us to live? Perhaps he will ask too much of us. Or push us away. And... and... well, we can come up with all sorts of excuses, which is why we so rarely experience Jesus' embrace in the here and now.

Oh, who is that coming through the door? It's Jesus! Jesus is here!

How will you respond?

✻ *Jesus, I can easily come up with all sorts of excuses to avoid simply trusting you, opening myself up to you, running to you with no strings attached, "trusting and expectant." Melt those excuses in the power of your Spirit today. Let me run to you as a child, with the open, vulnerable faith of one who utterly, utterly trusts you.*

thirty-five

THE SPRING WITHIN

> Jesus said, "Everyone who drinks this water will get thirsty again and again. Anyone who drinks the water I give will never thirst—not ever. The water I give will be an artesian spring within, gushing fountains of endless life."
>
> The woman said, "Sir, give me this water so I won't ever get thirsty, won't ever have to come back to this well again!"
>
> (John 4:13–15)

The woman at the well didn't quite get it. She was focused on her urgent, real, physical need for water. Wouldn't it be convenient to never have to carry heavy water jugs to the community well in the heat of the day? But Jesus was not speaking, of course, of physical thirst. We will always face physical needs, experience harsh situations, struggle with emotional upheaval and unexpected trauma. That is life.

The water Jesus offers is an eternal spring of the Spirit, "gushing fountains of endless life," forever slaking the thirst of deep spiritual need, because Jesus would be bubbling up inside us always, no matter what we faced in this earthly life. What are you thirsty for today?

- answers?
- insight?
- purpose?
- satisfaction?
- assurance?
- life?
- hope?
- relief?
- healing?
- money?
- clarity?
- love?

Some of those needs are simply part of the fabric of human life on earth. Others can be met through the fountain of spiritual reality Jesus promises to give you when you allow yourself to experience his love, when you live fully, every day, as one who is loved. Resting in God's presence. Confident, assured of your place in his heart.

When Jesus is within you, providing his special artesian spring water, you can face anything life throws at you. Is that too broad a promise? Does this really work? If it's true, why don't more people experience these "gushing fountains of endless life"?

Perhaps our expectations are askew. Look at Jesus' own life and you'll see that his promise doesn't necessarily translate into nonstop flowers and puppy dogs and a life in which nothing goes wrong. Review the lives and deaths of his closest followers and you'll see that Jesus' love isn't a lucky charm or a secret to surefire success. So why do we, at least unconsciously, expect that?

Keep the big picture in mind—the eternal, unending picture of grace and victory, of endless life in God's presence as well as in connection with other brothers and sisters in community. Discover ways to tap into that eternal life in the here-and-now by taking time to just stop and be, to converse with Jesus, and to let God's Spirit refresh you and empower you before you have to get back into the grit and grime of temporal life in this difficult world.

The woman had to go back to the well to satisfy her physical thirst. We too will have to take care of our physical and emotional needs while we live here on earth. But there is an artesian spring within.

Can you hear it splashing? Come take a deep drink and experience Jesus' love right now.

❋ *Jesus, I am thirsty. Thirsty for you. You offer eternal refreshment to my soul. I want it. Fill me with your bubbling presence, your gushing fountains of endless life. May I experience that effervescent love through the day today. Thank you.*

thirty-six

WHAT COUNTS BEFORE GOD

Jesus said, "But the time is coming—it has, in fact, come—when what you're called will not matter and where you go to worship will not matter.

"It's who you are and the way you live that count before God. Your worship must engage your spirit in the pursuit of truth. That's the kind of people the Father is out looking for: those who are simply and honestly *themselves* before him in their worship. God is sheer being itself—Spirit. Those who worship him must do it out of their very being, their spirits, their true selves, in adoration." (John 4:23–24)

I once had a phone conversation with a minister I would meet in person a few months later when he would come to record some sermons for our radio program, *Day1.* I didn't know much about him, although he'd been highly recommended and had preached on our program some time before I came on board as executive producer.

He and I had a delightful chat, talking about our families and ministries and backgrounds, getting to know each other. We seemed to relate naturally, bonding almost immediately. We talked on the phone and kept in touch by email in the following weeks before the recording session.

As we talked I created a mental image of this man. So, when he showed up at our studio, I was a surprised to see that my mental image was quite different from reality. In fact, he was much older than he sounded on the phone. But then I realized his spirit was young and vigorous, probably more so than mine! Over the years, our friendship has deepened, and he has become a loving mentor. I still thoroughly enjoy our occasional phone conversations, which always end with mutual expressions of love.

In that experience I learned something about our human responses to other people. We tend to describe ourselves in all sorts of ways, based on the stripes of our faith, our political views, our physical appearance or age, our relationships, our heritage, our race, our sexual orientation, whatever. White, married, middle-aged, moderate male. Retired, African-American, evangelical mother. Single, young, charismatic, Asian professional. Progressive Latino Catholic activist.

In fact, Jesus talked with the woman at the well about some of those labels—pointing out how they create barriers and divisions. Samaritan and Jew. Christian and Muslim. Republican and Democrat. Evangelical and mainline. Rich and poor. Straight and gay. Old and young. Red and blue. On and on. But as we experience the love of God through Christ, those labels—which tend to separate us—can dissolve in the reality of the Spirit, who binds all believers into one body, who makes all believers brothers and sisters, children of God, through Jesus Christ.

Jesus says the time is coming when those labels won't matter. In fact, that time is here. But maybe we don't realize it. We certainly don't experience it very often.

The only thing that matters to God, Jesus says, is who you are and how you live. God transcends all those aspects of human life that we generate into labels. God is Spirit, and God relates to our spirit, above and beyond the labels.

The key to any loving relationship is being simply and honestly yourself. If we want to experience God's love for us, we must approach him out of our very being, out of our true self.

That's how Jesus relates to us and how we relate to Jesus. And that's how we can relate to others as well.

Do you dare risk that today? It helps to spend some time first worshiping and adoring your God, simply and honestly.

❋ *Jesus, thank you for loving me for who I am—no matter who I am. Help me to see others as you see them—beyond the labels and distinctions that might separate us. Help me to reach out as a channel of your love and build bridges of faith in the Spirit.*

thirty-seven

NO SECRETS

Many of the Samaritans from that village committed themselves to him because of the woman's witness: "He knew all about the things I did. He knows me inside and out!"

(John 4:39)

Who in your life knows you best? Your spouse? A friend? A parent? A sibling? Do you know them as well as they know you? Or are you both kidding yourselves?

If we live with someone long enough, that person gets to know us inside and out, anticipating our moods, honoring (or at least putting up with) our routines, and sometimes even communicating with us without words. But sometimes we may hide things we have done, even from those closest to us, out of fear of rejection. We fear how people will react if they know the entire truth about us, so we keep some things secret.

This was true about the father of a woman I heard about. She thought she knew her father as well as a child could. But as a young adult she discovered that he'd had a previous marriage, one he had put totally behind him when he married her mother. She even had a half-brother and other relatives she had no idea existed. Her father had managed to keep this secret for years. I can't help but wonder how he felt when his secret was discovered.

And we all know someone in our circle of family and friends who, after years of living in fear of being found out, decided to live authentically and honestly as gay or lesbian. In some cases they make the decision to come out themselves; in others the truth is discovered by accident.

We never have to fear how God will react to the things in our life that we are afraid to bring out into the open. After all, look at how he treated the woman at the well. After one conversation with Jesus, the Samaritan woman felt he knew everything about her. Totally. The good, the bad, and the ugly. And yet he accepted her.

Do you struggle with past experiences you want to keep buried? Or secrets you hope no one discovers? Or embarrassing thoughts or unreasonable dreams? Are you trying to keep them from Jesus too? You might as well come clean, because you already are clean, as far as Jesus is concerned.

He knows you. Every part of you. Don't let that truth feel like a threat. It is an invitation to experience Jesus' love, to relate in a totally open, honest, free way with the lover of your soul—with no secrets, no reservations, no holding back.

❋ *Jesus, I come to you surrendering the secrets and fears I harbor, realizing you already know and understand and accept me totally. Thank you for loving me in spite of myself. Help me to be as honest and direct with you as you always are with me.*

thirty-eight

TRYING A NEW WAY

One man had been an invalid there for thirty-eight years. When Jesus saw him stretched out by the pool and knew how long he had been there, he said, "Do you want to get well?"

> The sick man said, "Sir, when the water is stirred, I don't have anybody to put me in the pool. By the time I get there, somebody else is already in."
>
> Jesus said, "Get up, take your bedroll, start walking." The man was healed on the spot. He picked up his bedroll and walked off. (John 5:5–9)

For thirty-eight years, this poor invalid had tried to get healed. Every day for all those years, all he could think about was how he could be the first person dunked in the healing Pool of Siloam whenever the water was divinely stirred. And for thirty-eight years, no one would help him to get into the waters.

Thirty-eight years!

Then Jesus walked by, spotted him, and asked him a rather obvious question. Finally! Someone noticed him. Maybe this fellow would help him into the pool.

No. Instead, Jesus opened the man's eyes to another way.

The man had worn blinders for so many years. He simply could not see any other option for his life: It was either get into that stirred-up pool or remain an invalid. It took Jesus' direct order to "get up, take your bedroll, and start walking" to shake this man out of his helpless, defeated, narrow-minded stupor.

Maybe you respond to this story the same way I usually do: that poor man. No one would help him for thirty-eight years. And then I realize how long I've been sitting beside my own little pool of unreached dreams. How long I've been thinking that my particular solutions to the problems that face me are the only ones that make sense. How long I've been frustrated that my answers never quite make it. So close! But the problems persist. You know the definition of insanity: doing the same thing over and over again while expecting a different result.

Then Jesus walks by. Do I notice him? Do I wonder if he is my ticket to whatever it is I want? Do I hope he will push me into the pool of the-way-I-think-things-should-be?

Jesus will have none of that. He rips the blinders off my eyes and takes me in a totally different direction. He proposes a stunningly different solution, one that had never even occurred to me. The invalid man thought that what he wanted was to get into that Pool of Siloam before anyone else. But Jesus reminded him that what he really wanted went beyond that. What he really wanted was to get well. But he had limited himself to only one solution—one that hadn't worked for thirty-eight years.

So, what do you think you want?

This vignette reminds us that we ought not get caught up in our cleverly devised solutions to our needs, the ones that are continually thwarted and unrealized. Maybe our solution to life's malaise is getting a particular job, or having a particular person in our life, or becoming rich or famous. Maybe our solution is safe and ordinary and unchallenging, or maybe it's simply impossible. The problem is, it's our solution, not God's.

We must get beyond our surface wants, beyond our shortsighted solutions, and realize our truest, deepest desire: to experience Jesus' love by knowing and serving him utterly. And maybe the way that plays out in our life is completely different than we ever imagined. We thought it would look like getting dunked in a pool, but Jesus calls us to something we never even considered.

What traditions have you so tied up that you are missing the release of Jesus' healing, that you never quite experience his love? What problems do you keep trying to solve in the same old ways? What questions keep gnawing at your soul when the answer is right in front of you, within reach of a simple step of faith? What fears and hurts have you kept protected from the healing love of Christ?

The process of experiencing Jesus' love starts by addressing a simple question from Jesus: "What do you want?" Get clear about it. Speak it. Then listen, really listen, to Jesus' response.

❋ *Jesus, I sometimes get so caught up in the expected, the traditional, the customary, the accepted, that I miss out on your unique provision of healing and love for me. Open my heart to your direct invitation to be healed and give me the courage to accept it.*

thirty-nine
THE SAVIOR'S APPRENTICE

> Jesus explained, "I'm telling you this straight. The Son can't independently do a thing, only what he sees the Father doing. What the Father does, the Son does. The Father loves the Son and includes him in everything he is doing.
>
> "But you haven't seen the half of it yet, for in the same way that the Father raises the dead and creates life, so does the Son. The Son gives life to anyone he chooses. Neither he nor the Father shuts anyone out. The Father handed all authority to judge over to the Son so that the Son will be honored equally with the Father. Anyone who dishonors the Son, dishonors the Father, for it was the Father's decision to put the Son in the place of honor." (John 5:19–23)

As a young adult I lived and worked in a small town for a few years. I remember once talking to a fellow member of a civic club over dinner. Though I had not met Bill before, I knew he was a successful businessman and pillar of the community. When he handed me his business card I noticed that, while he was listed as the president of his firm, the company was named after someone else—same last name as his, but a different first name. Of course, I assumed he must have followed his father in the family business.

Bill acknowledged that the name on the insurance firm's door was his father's. "But my father was never an insurance salesman," he explained. "He was a school teacher. He never made much money, but he worked as hard as he could and saved money so I could go to college. The truth is, he was my mentor, I was his apprentice—not for the insurance business, but for living life. He taught me, through his own example, how to treat others with respect and honor. How to put my own needs and wants after other people's. How to help out whenever I could, even sacrificially, when someone was in need. I learned so much about life and love from my father that, when I opened my own business, I put his name on the door instead of mine, as a way to honor him and the impact he had on my life. The things I learned from him, I wanted to put into practice in my business—and my life."

No wonder Bill had become a shining light in the community. He grew up with a father who loved him, knew him, communicated with him regularly, and taught him. He lived loved.

That's the kind of relationship Jesus has with the Father, and it's the kind of relationship you can have with Jesus. Through your study of his life, you can pay attention to how he reaches out to hurting people, how he handles sudden crises, how he copes with divisive issues. You can watch how he cares for those who trust him, how he accepts those who are different, how he stands up to injustice. In short, you can become Jesus' attentive apprentice, so you can learn how to live and love.

When that happens, there's no telling what God can do through you. In fact, "you haven't seen the half of it yet."

❋ *Jesus, I want to be your apprentice. As you learned how to live and love from your Father, I want to learn from you. Bring me into the circle of love and wisdom, so I might share that love and wisdom with all around me.*

forty

PAYING ATTENTION

Jesus explained, "You have your heads in your Bibles constantly because you think you'll find eternal life there. But you miss the forest for the trees. These Scriptures are all about *me!* And here I am, standing right before you, and you aren't willing to receive from me the life you say you want."

(John 5:39–40)

It's so easy to be distracted from the loving presence of Jesus in our lives. Some of those distractions are selfish and harmful, such as seeking love and fulfillment in places and people and ways that will never yield it.

Other distractions are positive and good, but they are still distractions. Jesus points to one: the Scriptures. That may sound surprising coming from Jesus' lips. There is certainly nothing wrong—and many things right—with studying the Word of God. But what is my purpose, my motive, in doing so?

- Am I just trying to nail down all the theological arguments in nice, neat little packages, so I don't have to struggle with my doubts or stretch myself in faith?
- Am I working to find all the right answers so I can debate others more knowledgeably?
- Am I simply attempting to occupy my time and fill the empty spaces in my heart with something that seems productive and positive?
- Am I engaging in an activity to find acceptance by other like-minded believers?
- Am I struggling to find life by unlocking the secret codes and mysteries supposedly found in the pages of the Bible?

Or am I searching the Scriptures to encounter the living Lord Christ? Am I opening my mind and heart and spirit to the work of the Holy Spirit through the printed word? Am I seeking to know the One who stands right before me, who lives within me? Am I using the Bible as a catalyst for real life, for true presence?

Jesus begs us not to let ourselves be distracted, not even by what seems to be good and positive. He is calling you to pay attention to him—to experience his loving presence—because he is alive. He is standing with you right now.

Jesus, I confess I get so distracted by doing, and that prevents me from being with you—the source of all life and love. Open my eyes. Make me more aware of your constant presence, your desire to give me the life I yearn to experience. Thank you for getting my attention.

forty-one

STRETCHABLE FAITH

> When Jesus looked out and saw that a large crowd had arrived, he said to Philip, "Where can we buy bread to feed these people?" He said this to stretch Philip's faith. He already knew what he was going to do. (John 6:5–6)

Some time ago I was wrestling with a critically important decision, one that would affect a lot of people and perhaps even the course of my future. I was talking about it via instant messaging online with a close friend. He lived far away from me but has always been one of the most honest, affirming, and loving people in my life. He told me:

> Don't give up. Be strong. Be confident.
> Make a good decision. Then . . . go.
> Life is too short. Before you die,
> why don't you do something that you love?

I had known the answer to my dilemma all along. I had spent months—years really—debating it and wrestling with it internally, feeling as though I was trying to figure it out, get it right, make the wisest, truest decision that would reflect the reality God has for me. But I guess I just didn't trust God enough to go with it. I didn't want my faith stretched so far—until my friend's lovingly direct challenge resonated in my heart.

This is often the case when it comes to major decisions. True, we face some decisions in which we really don't have a clue about what would be best. Other times our own expectations, wrong beliefs, or shortsightedness interfere with our ability to hear God's voice.

But in so many cases, I really did know, deep down, and I knew that I knew. Yet I had to spend weeks or months or even years struggling with it, trying to build up enough courage to follow it through, trying to figure it all out, considering the alternatives, posing questions, seeking advice, getting caught up in doubts, fearing what might happen if I actually did it, and then, finally, letting my faith be stretched enough to live out that decision in day-to-day life.

I think this process of moving from knowing to faith-stretching wrestling to actual resolution shows us a little about how Jesus works within us. When the Spirit moves on us to direct our lives in fresh and powerful ways, we know. But we tend to be too scared, too wary, too uncertain of the outcome to simply leap into it. We keep our faith too tightly constrained in the fear that maybe we aren't really hearing what we're hearing. We work very hard at protecting ourselves from the fear of the unknown. At least that's usually been my *modus operandi.*

But, as we see in the case of the feeding of the thousands with bread and fish, this process, according to Jesus, has a purpose: to help us to think outside the box of our own expectations, to help us to be open to a whole different scenario than we thought possible, to stretch our faith.

Jesus already knows what he is going to do in us and through us. Often, we do too. But we have to let Jesus stretch our faith so we can get there and actually do it.

❋ *Jesus, I think over the issues, the choices, the decisions I am wrestling with, and I see you already there, loving me, pushing me, coaxing me forward. I know it's a process—one I have to undertake to fully enter in. Enable me to follow through on your will in my life, no matter the cost, knowing that you are with me, loving me, always.*

forty-two

UNEXPECTED GRACE

In the evening his disciples went down to the sea, got in the boat, and headed back across the water to Capernaum. It had grown quite dark and Jesus had not yet returned. A huge

> wind blew up, churning the sea. They were maybe three or four miles out when they saw Jesus walking on the sea, quite near the boat. They were scared senseless, but he reassured them, "It's me. It's all right. Don't be afraid." So they took him on board. In no time they reached land—the exact spot they were headed to. (John 6:16–21)

Several months ago I was in New York City—huge, overwhelmingly busy, and extremely confusing to someone not familiar with its eccentricities. Take the subway system. If you know where you're going, you can figure it out. If you're not sure, you may never escape the bowels of the city.

I was staying for a meeting in a hotel on the border between Soho and Chinatown, and I had to make a relatively short subway ride to the Rector Street Station, just behind Trinity Episcopal Church on Wall Street and a block or two away from Ground Zero. I knew which letters of the subway I could take to get there—N or R—and the direction to go. Outside the subway stop, the signs at the top of the stairs descending from the sidewalk assured me I was in the right place. But once I had paid my fare and gotten to the waiting area, I realized that none of the signs indicated that the train I wanted would be stopping there.

I panicked. I've found New Yorkers can be friendly enough to provide directions to hapless out-of-towners like me, and I have benefited from that generous tendency more than once. But that morning I was harried, nervous about the day's meetings, and feeling too insecure to ask. So I started wandering. Up and down stairways, along tiled corridors, trying to find a subway sign that made some sense to me.

After some minutes of crawling around underground, I finally found what I thought was the right platform. Still feeling anxious and lost, surrounded by busy, unaware New Yorkers heading to work or school or wherever, I glanced behind me and saw a friend who was heading to the same meeting I was.

Was I glad to see him! I told him that now that he—who was much more expert in the vagaries of the New York subway system—was there, I knew I was in the right place. That friend, in a small but not inconsequential sense, was Jesus to me in that moment.

Jesus tends to pop up unexpectedly in places where we desperately need him, as he did to the disciples. They were fearing for their lives in a storm—and then fearing for their sanity when they saw him walking toward them on the roiling surface of the angry lake to reassure them of his presence. They weren't expecting him to show up, particularly like that. But that is often Jesus' way. He pushes his way into our most stormy, frightening, lost moments to show us the way, to give us hope, to hear him say, "It's me. It's all right. Don't be afraid."

He does that because he loves us, and he wants us to know it.

❋ *Jesus, help me to trust that you will truly be exactly where I need you most, when I need you most. In the midst of the storms and rolling seas of the stresses and problems and fears of my life, be present. Calm the sea. Calm me. Take me where I am going safe and sound.*

forty-three

OUT OF THE SHALLOWS

> Jesus answered, "You've come looking for me not because you saw God in my actions but because I fed you, filled your stomachs—and for free.
>
> "Don't waste your energy striving for perishable food like that. Work for the food that sticks with you, food that nourishes your lasting life, food the Son of Man provides. He and what he does are guaranteed by God the Father to last."
>
> (John 6:26–27)

We can be so easily satisfied, yet so impossible to please. Jesus had performed a miracle in feeding so many hungry people with bread and fish. They were excited about him, eager to see what trick he would perform next, anxious to have their frivolous hungers alleviated in surprising ways. But they were missing the point.

And so can we. We pray for the money we need to cover some unexpected expense. Or we seek swift healing from a minor ailment. Or we beg Jesus for a quick, easy resolution to a conflict with someone we're close to.

God may provide answers to these prayers, and when that happens we can check them off and move on. But more often, I think, God doesn't let us get away with that. God wants us to go past the surface, beyond the simple answers, the full stomachs, the easy solutions.

God doesn't want us to be satisfied merely with the basics, simply meeting our physical needs with a piece of bread and fish. He wants us to dive into the depths of lasting life, to hunger for the food the Son of Man provides. The food of hard-won maturity and wisdom. The food of self-sacrificial obedience. The food of working to fulfill the calling God has given to us.

This food is not necessarily sweet. It's hard to chew. And without the experience of Christ's love, it's even harder to swallow.

Jesus wants us to pursue this kind of life. It takes work. It takes time. It takes deep desire. It means rearranging priorities and questioning our goals. It means sacrificing some of the comforts the rest of our world enjoys and giving ourselves the opportunity to bask in Christ's presence, experience his love, and listen to his call on our hearts.

We may never feel that we "get there," that we fully experience satisfaction in our souls, because we are always striving for more of Jesus. We always feel that we could be more for him. But this is how we experience his presence—his rich, filling, nourishing, lasting, loving presence.

❋ *Jesus, I'm starving. I realize I try to fill my hunger with the trite, the shallow—with life's fast food. You are calling me to a different sort of diet: the nourishment of your love that challenges me and pushes me and stretches me and lasts forever. I hear you say, "Take, eat."*

forty-four

TRUSTING THE PROCESS

> Jesus said, "I came down from heaven not to follow my own whim but to accomplish the will of the One who sent me.
>
> "This, in a nutshell, is that will: that everything handed over to me by the Father be completed—not a single detail missed—and at the wrap-up of time I have everything and everyone put together, upright and whole. This is what my Father wants: that anyone who sees the Son and trusts who he is and what he does and then aligns with him will enter *real* life, *eternal* life. My part is to put them on their feet alive and whole at the completion of time." (John 6:38–40)

Many years ago, I attended a weekend retreat led by a gifted psychotherapist who later became a friend, mentor, and hero of mine. A half-dozen or so people had gathered in a rustic cabin in southwest Georgia to get down to some intense and personal emotional and spiritual work. It would stretch us and enable God to work in us in amazing, unique ways. I knew that each of us would work individually with the psychotherapist on a mat on the floor, opening our wounded hearts as he peeled back layers of pain to help us to understand and deal with our problems. But how that actually worked and what would happen when I was on the mat, I had no idea.

As I entered the retreat center on that Friday evening, I was anxious. I knew nobody there—although one fellow I knew by sight as a member of the church I belonged to. Some of them had been to these retreats before; I was one of the new ones. I didn't know what I was in for, but I knew it would be challenging and even frightening. Then I spotted a sign on the wall that read simply: "Trust the process."

I wasn't entirely sure what the process was, but I determined to trust it, to enter in, to let the Spirit of God take me wherever I was supposed to go. And that weekend turned out to be the most freeing and cleansing time I think I have ever experienced, and it started me on a long path toward becoming who God created me to be. I see that weekend as an analogy of sorts to the life lived in the experience of Christ's love. It's not just a couple of days; it's the rest of our lives.

You see, if you love Jesus, if you seek to experience his love and be fully the person God has created you to be, you are in a lifelong process of change and growth. When you see Jesus, trust who he is and what he does, and determine to walk alongside him, you begin a process that takes your entire life and leads you to glory. But there are some hard truths about this process.

This process may not feel good. It can be painful and messy and confusing and downright scary at times. And the more you risk in following Christ radically, the more painful, messy, confusing, and scary it can be. It forces you to trust the one who says he loves you.

This process may not make sense. You are seeking God's will for you. In Jesus' case, the Father's will led to the cross, which, on the surface, looked like a failure. What God leads you to do may at times make people question your sanity. What's worse, it may not make sense to you, either. But if you are truly open to Christ's loving guidance, it will.

This process may cost you a lot in terms of your time, your priorities, your gifts, your possessions, even your relationships. You will continually have to ask yourself, "Is it worth it?" Yes, Jesus says, it is—but you must trust that.

This process may seem overwhelming at times. You keep telling yourself God will not give you more than you can bear, but it sure feels like God takes you right up hard against that line. It seems impossible. But if it didn't, God wouldn't be in it.

This process ultimately has a happy ending. It may not be what we anticipated as "happy," but it's the right ending. That's part of the deal between the Father and the Son. Jesus says his job is to have "everyone put together, upright and whole"; his part is "to put them on their feet alive and whole at the completion of time."

How alive and whole are you feeling right now?

Maybe not very. But that's okay. You are in the flow of this loving process, right where you need to be. Trust it. Jesus is with you every step of the way into real life, eternal life.

❋ *Jesus, I step back and look at the path you've put me on—the one that leads to real life, eternal life. I see the steep hills and the low valleys, the treacherous parts and the boring parts. And I see you walking with me every step of the way. Help me to stay on this path with you. Help me to trust the process.*

forty-five

A LOVING FORGIVENESS

The religion scholars and Pharisees led in a woman who had been caught in an act of adultery. They stood her in plain sight of everyone and said, "Teacher, this woman was caught red-handed in the act of adultery. Moses, in the Law, gives orders to stone such persons. What do you say?" They were trying to trap him into saying something incriminating so they could bring charges against him.

Jesus bent down and wrote with his finger in the dirt. They kept at him, badgering him. He straightened up and said, "The sinless one among you, go first: Throw the stone." Bending down again, he wrote some more in the dirt.

Hearing that, they walked away, one after another, beginning with the oldest. The woman was left alone. Jesus stood up and spoke to her. "Woman, where are they? Does no one condemn you?"

"No one, Master."

"Neither do I," said Jesus. "Go on your way. From now on, don't sin." (John 8:3–11)

When those who are deeply hurt are able to forgive those who hurt them, it makes news. Even this morning, as I pondered this passage from John's gospel, a newspaper headline caught my eye: "Brutal crime, then forgiveness." The story was about a random killing of a twenty-year-old man by four other young men between the ages of sixteen and twenty-one. It was senseless. The police termed it a "random act of violence."

After the four suspects were brought into court, one of the suspect's aunts walked over to two sisters of the victim. "My son wants you to know that he apologizes," she said as all eyes filled with tears, "even though he didn't do the shooting, and that he will cooperate with the police and do what is right."

"Apology accepted," one of the sisters whispered back. They embraced in the courtroom.[13]

You may need to hear this today: Your sin is forgiven. Apology accepted.

Whether it's caught-in-the-act adultery, hypocritical judgmentalism, cowardly faith, an innocently broken commandment, or random violence, Jesus forgives sin. When we realize and accept his forgiveness, he sets us free to live in a new way—the way of the forgiven.

Not that there won't be consequences. The forgiven young man in the newspaper story could well face years of incarceration. In other cases, marriages may be broken. Wounds may never fully heal. Scars may not fade.

But hearts can be remade. If we allow ourselves to live in that forgiveness, to live as one loved fully and totally without reservation, our life can gain new meaning.

Tom Wright makes an insightful comment that can help us to grasp a significant distinction here:

> Jesus' last words to the woman are extremely important. If she has been forgiven—if she's been rescued from imminent death—she must live by that forgiveness. Forgiveness is not the same as "tolerance." Being forgiven doesn't mean that sin doesn't matter. On the contrary: "forgiveness" means that sin does matter—but that God is choosing to set it aside.[14]

Each of us must confess that we have messed up countless times in our lives, and this behavior has hurt countless people—physically, emotionally, even spiritually. But if we recognize that God has forgiven us, if we can learn to live in that forgiveness and be set free from the guilt we have earned, then we can go forward in life, making a positive rather than negative impact in others' lives.

We don't know what happened to the woman Jesus forgave, the woman he told to "go on your way [and] don't sin." But we do know that Jesus saw her heart and that he can see our hearts, too. He is well aware of what we've done and why we've done it, and of how desperately we want to rise above all that, make amends, and start over.

He's willing to give us that chance. If we'll take it.

❋ *Jesus, I fall at your feet knowing I am a sinner, shocked at the fact that you would love me enough to forgive me. Thank you for giving me a fresh start—and the power to walk with you in new strength and purpose.*

forty-six

SHINING THE LIGHT

> Jesus once again addressed them: "I am the world's Light. No one who follows me stumbles around in the darkness. I provide plenty of light to live in." (John 8:12)

Years ago I heard a story about some people who were trapped in an office building during a power outage. The elevators, of course, did not work, and the office workers were instructed to go down the stairs. Unfortunately, there were no emergency lights, so total darkness engulfed the people in the stairwells. Slowly, each person tried to feel each step in the stairwell. Many of them lost their balance and knocked several others down with them.

After a few minutes of potential horror, one of the men remembered that the face of his wristwatch glowed when he pushed in the stem. Remarkably, he was able to lead the group of people from the upper floors safely down the stairs using the faint glow of his wristwatch to light the way.

Even the light of a single candle can shatter the darkness. But Jesus' light is far brighter and warmer than a glowing wristwatch or a flickering candle. Because he loves us,

- He shines the light of healing on the dark areas of pain and need in our hearts.
- He shines the light of hope in the dark spaces of fear in our souls.
- He shines the light of wisdom in the dark places of doubt and uncertainty and ignorance.
- He shines the light of forgiveness in the dark corners of sin we try to keep out of sight.
- He shines the light of love in the dark holes of emptiness and hate and anger we keep hidden within us.

Jesus is the light of the whole world. When we are with him, experiencing his love, we don't need to stumble around in the world's darkness. We have all the light we need to live.

But we must open our eyes to see it. We must acknowledge the darkness surrounding us—the darkness of pain or fear or doubt—and then open it up to Jesus' loving light, asking for his wisdom, his clarity, his bright reality.

Jesus' light is warm and inviting—and it is shining on you right now. Can you see it?

❋ *Jesus, sometimes the world feels so dark. And my heart feels even darker. But you are the Lord of light, and you love me. Shine your light of healing, hope, wisdom, forgiveness, and love on me, in me, through me. Shine!*

forty-seven
TRUE FREEDOM

> Then Jesus turned to the Jews who had claimed to believe in him. "If you stick with this, living out what I tell you, you are my disciples for sure. Then you will experience for yourselves the truth, and the truth will free you." . . .
>
> Jesus said, "I tell you most solemnly that anyone who chooses a life of sin is trapped in a dead-end life and is, in fact, a slave. A slave is a transient, who can't come and go at will. The Son, though, has an established position, the run of the house. So if the Son sets you free, you are free through and through." (John 8:31–32, 34–36)

Sometimes I wear a silver ring purchased several years ago in Edinburgh, Scotland, while visiting that wild and beautiful land. Etched on the face of the ring is the Wallace family crest—a raised, armored arm grasping a sword, with the motto *Pro Libertate* (For Freedom) circling it.

The motto arose out of the efforts of William Wallace to free Scotland from English rule, a heroic story recounted in the movie *Braveheart*. If you've seen that movie, you may remember Mel Gibson leading his ragtag band with the rallying cry, "Freedom!"

The Scots thirsted for freedom from tyranny, freedom to rule themselves, and freedom from political slavery. Eventually, the nation did experience that freedom—for a time. A decade ago the rallying cry rose again for Scotland to declare independence from the United Kingdom. They didn't exactly get that, but they did get their own parliament. And they keep trying to gain full independence.

Deep within every human heart lies the desire for freedom. But this desire goes beyond the political or economic realm. We seek freedom from death. Freedom from slavery. Freedom from meaninglessness. Freedom from emptiness. Freedom from sin. Freedom from lovelessness.

We yearn to experience that freedom. All it takes, Jesus says, is "living out what I tell you." Making Jesus' ways part of the fabric of our being. Staying in Christ's loving embrace through the day. The alternative is to be trapped in the dead-end life of slavery to our own desires, needs, and false hopes.

But notice who Jesus is addressing here: those "who had claimed to believe in him." You see, there's a difference between claiming to believe in Jesus and actually, fully, authentically believing in him. It's the difference between slavery and freedom. We may believe in Christ, we may have put our full faith in him, but that doesn't automatically enable us to experience freedom from the power of sin. That takes a lifetime of getting to know Jesus, experiencing his love, and living in the freedom he alone provides.

Are you experiencing Jesus' freedom through and through? If not, consider how authentically you believe in him.

❋ *Jesus, in your loving presence, in living out what you tell me, I find freedom from my slavery to self and to sin. Give me the faith to believe that, to experience it, and to share it today.*

forty-eight

THROUGH THE GATE

Jesus said, "I am the Gate for the sheep. All those others are up to no good—sheep stealers, every one of them. But the sheep didn't listen to them. I am the Gate. Anyone who goes through me will be cared for—will freely go in and out, and find pasture. A thief is only there to steal and kill and destroy. I came so they can have real and eternal life, more and better life than they ever dreamed of." (John 10:7–10)

I once read about a doorman who worked at the same building in Manhattan for dozens of years. On the eve of his retirement, he was interviewed about his life experience as one who opened the door for so many New Yorkers. What struck me was his faithful service, even when he was essentially ignored. People would come and go, many of them so self-important they just walked through the open door without even a thank-you nod. A large number of them, however, came to appreciate him and often would chat with him as friends.

Regardless, he said, he came to know most everyone who lived in that building better than perhaps they knew themselves. As he did his job, he listened and observed carefully—not to be nosy, but to try to serve them better.

I think of that faithful doorman every time I read this passage. Commentators tell us that in Jesus' time, shepherds would guard their flocks at night by lying across the opening of the pen, serving personally as the gate. That way they could watch over their sheep, ensure their safety, keep them in for rest and protection, and let them out for pasture and exercise.

Jesus says he does the same with his followers. As a true shepherd, Jesus has the best in mind for us, his loving followers. He came to give us something we could have no other way, something we yearn for from the depths of our being. He came to give us "real and eternal life, more and better life" than we could ever dream of. But we must *first* find our place in the sheep pen, under his protective care.

What sort of life are you dreaming of? One marked by love and joy, by purpose and meaning, peace and fullness? That is the life Jesus wants you to experience, day by day, forever.

How can you experience it? Pay attention to Jesus as he works in your life. Be aware of the Spirit working out the rough edges of your life, calling you to deeper faithfulness, opening up opportunities to learn about yourself, about God, about serving others. Let him reach out to you when you need to be held, watched over, protected and cared for, and filled with rest and peace.

And when you are ready, go through him, through the Gate and into the world, taking that same love and care and peace with you to share with others, always under his watchful eye. This is real life, eternal life, more and better life than you ever dreamed of.

❋ *Jesus, sometimes I strain against the idea of being one of your sheep. I want to run free, in my own way, in my own directions. Yet there are difficult consequences for that approach. Help me to find myself in your arms, as my loving shepherd. Give me a taste today of the abundant life you hold out for me in your care. And give me opportunities to share that life with others.*

forty-nine

A NEW LEVEL OF LIFE

Martha said, "Master, if you'd been here, my brother wouldn't have died. Even now, I know that whatever you ask God he will give you."

Jesus said, "Your brother will be raised up."

Martha replied, "I know that he will be raised up in the resurrection at the end of time."

"You don't have to wait for the End. I am, right now, Resurrection and Life. The one who believes in me, even though he or she dies, will live. And everyone who lives believing in me does not ultimately die at all. Do you believe this?" (John 11:21–26)

Word had gotten to Jesus of Lazarus's illness, but he delayed traveling to see his friend. When Jesus arrived, he found his friends, Lazarus's sisters, Mary and Martha, grieving. Lazarus was dead.

Martha knew Jesus, knew his power to perform miracles. But now it was too late. If only Jesus had come, he could have healed Lazarus of his illness. But Jesus would not be limited by her expectations. He had other plans. He wanted to do something for Lazarus that was far beyond what any of them could ever imagine. Jesus wanted to demonstrate that he could overturn death.

He gives life, and those who believe in him, who walk in his love, will live and never die. Starting right now. Life as God intends it—full of mystery and joy and challenge and love and extreme surprise—is possible when we experience Christ's love, now and forever.

But, like Martha, our expectations may be too low. We spend too much time muttering "If only..." and neglecting the possibilities right in front of us to live and serve and love in magnanimous, Spirit-led ways. We guard our hearts from the Spirit's invasion out of fear or ignorance or laziness or pride. We're in bondage to our boxed-in understanding of God's purpose for us. We get so comfortable in our routines and responsibilities and presuppositions that we don't even realize that Christ is trying to get our attention. We can't take our eyes off our spirit-tightening circumstances to look at the far horizon of heaven and the possibilities of a life of energizing freedom and radical fulfillment, a life of beyond-the-call service, a life of generously loving service for our Lord. We just assume we can't do it, can't afford it, have no time for it, or don't have the gift for it.

The last thing we expect is that the corpse of our dreary, meaningless life can be resurrected. But Jesus constantly surprises those who know him and follow him. His surprises take us to a new level of life—a radical new understanding of God's will for us. That fiery dream that lies so dormant in your memory—can it be rekindled? That dust-covered goal to do something so much bigger than you ever thought possible—can you take that to Jesus and ask him to raise it? That long-forgotten idea you had that seemed so crazy yet brilliant so long ago—is God's Spirit starting to breathe new life into it?

I have so far to go in raising my expectations of myself, but I look back at the times I dared to trust God to let me write a book or produce a radio program or make what felt like a costly donation to help someone in need or simply to reach out to a stranger—things I didn't think I could ever do, and certainly couldn't have done without a little resurrection power.

How about you? Jesus' Spirit pulls at us to go further, far beyond our comfort zone, to raise our expectations of ourselves and trust him for the impossible. And Jesus asks, "Do you believe this?"

✼ *Jesus, you are the Resurrection and the Life. You call me to a different plane of existence, realizing the reality of eternal life in this world. Surprise me today to remind me of your authority and your call on my life.*

fifty

HOW DEEPLY HE LOVED

> When Jesus saw Mary sobbing and the Jews with her sobbing, a deep anger welled up within him. He said, "Where did you put him?"
>
> "Master, come and see," they said. Now Jesus wept.
>
> The Jews said, "Look how deeply he loved him."
>
> (John 11:33–36)

When Jesus saw Mary and those around her crying their hearts out over the loss of Lazarus, he was deeply troubled, angry at the pain and suffering these dear people had to endure. And he burst into tears.

Yes, as this poignant story makes clear, Jesus was fully human, expressing real, human emotions. He loved his friends—Lazarus, who had died, as well as his sisters, Mary and Martha. But the message of this story—indeed, of John's gospel as a whole—goes much deeper than that, as Tom Wright points out:

> When we look at Jesus, *not least when we look at Jesus in tears,* we are seeing not just a flesh-and-blood human being but the Word made flesh (1.1–14). The Word, through whom the worlds were made, weeps like a baby

> at the grave of his friend. Only when we stop and ponder this will we understand the full mystery of John's gospel. Only when we put away our high-and-dry pictures of who God is and replace them with pictures in which the Word who is God can cry with the world's crying will we discover what the word "God" really means.[15]

Step back from this moving scene for a moment. Think about what makes you weep today. What breaks your heart? What stirs your fears, your grief, your sense of loss? What makes you angry over its unfairness? What pain sits like a boulder on your chest?

Think about those things . . . and see Jesus bursting into tears with you. Jesus loves you and can do all things for you in the Father's power. Your loving Savior is with you; he knows you, understands your pain, and sits with you in it—and he can do something with it.

Maybe he won't raise the dead you are grieving for. Maybe he won't change the circumstances you are struggling under or weeping about. Maybe he can't correct the social injustice that infuriates you as fast as you'd like. But he can give you new life, new hope, and new passion. He is with you, right where you are. Look how deeply he loves you.

❋ *Jesus, I do sense you with me, understanding my pain, sitting with me in my dark circumstances. Thank you for sharing your loving presence with me. Give me the hope and strength to endure and to grow through this into your glory.*

fifty-one
LET LOOSE

> Then Jesus shouted, "Lazarus, come out!" And he came out, a cadaver, wrapped from head to toe, and with a kerchief over his face.
>
> Jesus told them, "Unwrap him and let him loose."
>
> (John 11:43–44)

Just like Lazarus, you were dead until you met Jesus. You were wrapped in sin and self-absorption, trapped in a life with no future. Covered by fears and emptiness and futility. Bound by powerlessness. Then Jesus called your name, and you came out of the tomb of life-without-Jesus. You came alive. You walked out into a new world. It may have looked like the same old world, but this world has Jesus with you in it.

Notice what happened when Jesus raised Lazarus from the dead. Yes, Jesus called him by name. Yes, Lazarus was raised to life and walked out of his tomb. But he still needed the help of his family and friends, of the community of faith around him, to be set free.

Jesus directed Lazarus's family and friends and neighbors to come around him. He needed the community to unwrap the corpse-wear that bound him and to let him loose.

If you are seeking to experience Jesus' love, take note of this: you need community. Yes, Jesus can give you life, can raise you to a higher plane of existence. But you need the support and encouragement of the family of faith around you to unwrap your grave clothes and set you loose to follow Jesus freely.

I've found this need to be surrounded by a faith community to be beautifully fulfilled so often throughout my life. I was raised in the church; my father was a dedicated United Methodist minister. I grew up going to every service, learning about God, seeing how life was supposed to be lived by observing the community around me. I can still remember the vacation Bible school class in which Mrs. Robinette first encouraged my passion to write. In college, I found another church community, with a group of people who both cared for me and challenged me as I started to answer God's call on my life. I even worked part-time for the warmly encouraging pastor as the church secretary for a year.

When I was set free into the world, yet another church became my home, challenging me to get involved in service in new ways—through Sunday school teaching, choir singing, and community service. The little United Church of Christ congregation I served as a student pastor in South Dallas while I was in seminary no longer exists, except in the hearts of those, like me, whom the community had touched. In recent years I've been a member of an Episcopal church that takes seriously its role of encouraging, teaching, listening, challenging, and walking with me.

If you have been in love with Jesus for some time, pay attention to what the story of Lazarus's community is telling you: Be part of a church body that surrounds and supports those who come into it, those seeking God's ways, those wanting to love and follow Jesus. Your role is to help those people get loose of the death-wrappings that have kept them stuck in the tomb of lifelessness.

Value the community of faith that has nurtured you, the community that you're now a part of, the community that provides a tangible way of experiencing Jesus' love. Being a part of the body of Christ is a vital part of the process of resurrection and eternal life.

❋ *Jesus, thank you for the reminder of the importance of the family of faith, the community of the church in my life. Thank you for telling me I can experience and share your love through the body of Christ. Show me how to be a more active and effective part of my community of faith, both to receive and to share the blessings of being together as people who love Jesus and who are called to follow him.*

fifty-two
STORM-TOSSED GLORY

Jesus said, "Right now I am storm-tossed. And what am I going to say? 'Father, get me out of this'? No, this is why I came in the first place. I'll say, 'Father, put your glory on display.'"
A voice came out of the sky: "I have glorified it, and I'll glorify it again." (John 12:27–28)

When I was growing up, my family spent nearly every summer at one of several cabins alongside the James River in the Tidewater area of Virginia. When the cabins were razed and the property turned into a riverside mobile-home resort, my folks bought a single-wide and moved right in.

After my dad retired, he and Mom spent half the year there, mere feet away from the river's shoreline. Occasionally, throughout all that time, a severe storm or even a hurricane would blow through. Almost every time some damage was sustained—the loss of some docks or boardwalk, some boats washed away, part of the shoreline eroded. But the little riverside community would work together to rebuild, and life would go on.

A few years ago, my folks sold their beachfront mobile home, and I felt a great loss because I loved that place. So many wonderful memories from childhood into adulthood were created there. Then a few years ago, hurricane Floyd hit the area and wiped out the entire community. My brother took some digital pictures of the destruction when he stopped by while traveling, and he sent them to the rest of the family. The scene was devastating, heart-breaking. Mere piles of rubble.

Maybe right now, as you read this, your life feels storm-tossed, as though it's been hit by a hurricane. Mine sure did not long ago. Everywhere I turned, it seemed, I faced a new question, an unexpected problem, even a crisis. It felt as though God was shaking me down to the very foundations of life, perhaps to build a new thing. Yet looking through it all—beyond the storm clouds—I could see the sun shining. I could see hope. I could see Jesus, who has already crossed the stormy seas ahead of me, his arms stretched toward me in welcoming love.

Sometimes in a storm, things get shaken loose. It's what we do with the rubble that matters. And only if we live knowing and experiencing God's love for us can we do much that's positive in the way of rearranging the rubble.

According to this passage, Jesus knows how we feel when events hit us with the force of a hurricane and our life is in shambles. He probably felt the distress a lot more deeply than we ever do, because his life was on the line. He knew he had to die, so he didn't ask for a quick escape, an easy out. Despite his painful doubts soon to come in the garden of Gethsemane, when he asked his Father to take the bitter cup away from him, still he knew this was why he had come to earth. He knew this tragic storm would bring glory to the Father, would reveal the Father's love and power to the whole world. It would open the way for each of us to experience the inexpressible love God has for us.

When you think about the storms Jesus endured, and when you realize he is with you in the midst of yours, maybe you can begin to catch a glimpse of God's glory as well.

Oh, by the way, they've cleaned up all the debris at that family resort on the banks of the James River. Something new is coming, better than it ever was.

❋ *Jesus, the wind blows cold through my heart at times, but the warmth of your presence reminds me of your constant love and care. Help me to hold on. And reveal the glory of God to me in places I never expected it.*

fifty-three

CHILDREN OF LIGHT

Jesus said, "For a brief time still, the light is among you. Walk by the light you have so darkness doesn't destroy you. If you walk in darkness, you don't know where you're going. As you have the light, believe in the light. Then the light will be within you, and shining through your lives. You'll be children of light." (John 12:35–36)

One evening when I was a teenager, I joined three friends for a typical do-nothing-and-hope-you-don't-get-into-trouble kind of time. One friend had a new Jeep Wrangler. At dusk we all climbed into the rough-riding vehicle and took off for the rural area outside our hometown.

We stopped for a snack—burgers and chili dogs and fries—then got back in the Jeep and sped along curving rural roads, joking and laughing. Our driver had the radio going and was talking away with us. He was squinting to see the road ahead. The stars were out, maybe a sliver of a moon, but suddenly he blurted in near exasperation, "Man, is it dark tonight!"

The rest of us agreed. It *was* mighty dark—and then one of us realized that our driver had forgotten to turn on the headlights. We hooted about that for miles.

Sometimes life seems very dark. Darker than usual. We can make out the edges of ordinariness, but can't quite get it into focus, can't quite navigate without feeling as though we're taking our life into our hands, foolishly moving forward in the dark. Sometimes it feels like the darkness can destroy us. We don't know where we are going.

Jesus acknowledges that feeling. But he also provides the light we need. We have to believe in the light, his light. We have to open our eyes and see it—by spending time with him in prayer and meditation, by letting his words and works marinate our soul. Then we can see. We can be children of light. We can share that light as doers and givers and lovers.

Jesus' warm and loving light shows us the way of grace and security. It enables us to take risky steps forward, because we can see more clearly where we are going. It keeps us safe and out of danger.

Jesus wants us not only to see the light, use the light, be blessed by the light, but also to share the light. To let it shine through our lives so others can see, so that together we can move forward and see where we're going.

Open your eyes. See the light. Jesus is there.

❋ *Jesus, sometimes the darkness smothers me with fear and uncertainty. Open my eyes and my heart to your light—the light of truth, of love, of justice. Let me live by that light and share it with others. Shine through me, Jesus.*

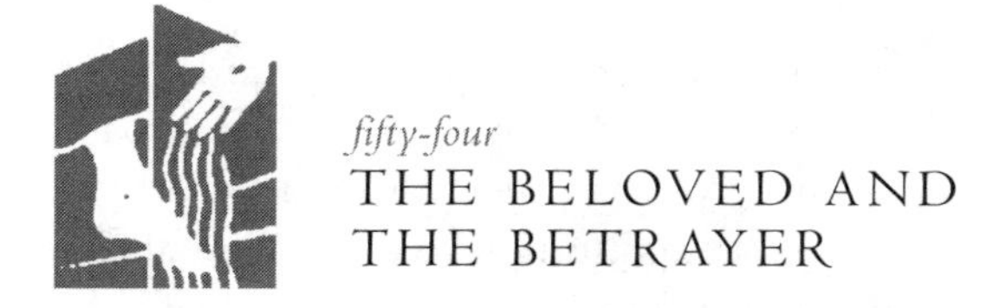

fifty-four

THE BELOVED AND THE BETRAYER

After he said these things, Jesus became visibly upset, and then he told them why. "One of you is going to betray me."

The disciples looked around at one another, wondering who on earth he was talking about. One of the disciples, the one Jesus loved dearly, was reclining against him, his head on his shoulder. Peter motioned to him to ask who Jesus might be talking about. So, being the closest, he said, "Master, who?"

Jesus said, "The one to whom I give this crust of bread after I've dipped it." Then he dipped the crust and gave it to Judas, son of Simon the Iscariot. As soon as the bread was in his hand, Satan entered him.

"What you must do," said Jesus, "do. Do it and get it over with." (John 13:21–27)

Tension. Suspicion. Fear. Betrayal. Gut-wrenching emotions fill this scene, which focuses on two disciples, two ways of life:

- *The betrayer—Judas.* Trusting his own way, willing to give up his friend and teacher for what he believed were greater ends.
- *And the beloved—John.* Reclining against Jesus, resting his head on his Master's shoulder, hearing the heartbeat of his loving friend, trusting in his love, and living loved in the safety of his embrace.

We don't know why Judas did what he did. Perhaps he had become disenchanted with the way of Jesus—with humble, loving service—and wanted him out of the way so a "true Messiah" could emerge to lead Israel to victory over Rome. Maybe he was putting Jesus to the test, hoping that if he were pressured to exert his divine authority, he would call down the angels of heaven to rescue him and bring in the kingdom. Whatever Judas's motives, as a result of his actions Jesus went to the cross.

But in the sweep of the drama of betrayal it is easy to lose sight of the image of the disciple Jesus loved dearly, reclining against him at the table, his head on Jesus' chest—a place of supreme trust and abandoned love. This image depicts the place we all yearn to be: close beside our loving Lord, fully present with him, no matter what is happening around us.

As Brennan Manning has so beautifully expressed it:

> John lays his head on the heart of God, on the breast of the Man whom the council of Nicea defined as "being coequal and consubstantial to the Father... God from God, Light from Light, True God from True God."... Have we ever seen the human Jesus at closer range? Clearly, John was not intimidated by Jesus. He was not afraid of his Lord and Master. John was deeply affected by this sacred Man.... As John leans back on the breast of Jesus and listens to the heartbeat of the Great Rabbi, he comes to know Him in a way that surpasses mere cognitive knowledge. What a world of difference lies

> between knowing about someone and knowing *Him!* In a flash of intuitive understanding, John experiences Jesus as the human face of the God who is love. And in coming to know who the Great Rabbi is, John discovers who he is—the disciple Jesus loved.[16]

This is the place for living loved. This is your place. Yet in saying that, we realize that we can never tangibly be in that place. Jesus no longer physically walks this earth. Neither you nor I are the young disciple in that upper room so many centuries ago.

And yet Jesus is just as close to you as he was to the beloved disciple. Closer, in fact. He is in you and around you and under you and beside you. But his Spirit-presence requires more of us than it did of John. John could lean against skin, feel the breath of the Master in his hair. But we have to be intentionally aware of Jesus' presence, acknowledge it, and live as though it were true. Because it is.

When we live in his love, experience it as real, and let it overflow our hearts and spread to others, there can be no doubt that we too are disciples that Jesus loves.

❋ *Jesus, I want to be with you, in your embrace, leaning against your chest, hearing your heartbeat, knowing your love. I want to experience that intimacy with you and to let it fill me with a sense of purpose, as I take that love to others in your name.*

fifty-five

WHEN JESUS FEELS ABSENT

> Jesus answered, "Don't let this throw you. You trust God, don't you? Trust me. There is plenty of room for you in my Father's home. If that weren't so, would I have told you that I'm on my way to get a room ready for you? And if I'm on my way to get your room ready, I'll come back and get you so you can live where I live." (John 14:1–3)

A friend once shared with me the story—and it's truly a love story—of his father and mother, Charlie and Jean. When they met, Charlie and Jean were smitten. They could barely function without each other. They thought they had to be together constantly. This belief affected every other aspect of their lives, of course—their education, their work, and their friendships. They were consumed with each other, but immaturely so.

Then Charlie was drafted into the army to fight in Vietnam. Just before he left, he promised his anguished young wife that he would return and they would live together. Both assumed they would return to the mutually smothering way of life they thought was the ultimate experience of life.

But Charlie's experiences as a soldier in Vietnam shaped him into a much more mature, thoughtful, and realistic person. Meanwhile, still relying on his love and waiting for his return, Jean learned how to be self-sufficient, finishing her education, launching a career, and supporting herself.

Neither could wait to return to the other's arms. But when that day finally arrived, they discovered each was in love with a totally different person. They had both grown immensely and, thankfully, their love had grown, too. It opened each of them up to the world around them.

Similarly, when we fall in love with Jesus, our love is often a self-centered, immature love. We wallow in the graces and the lavish blessings, and we can get stuck there. Perhaps that's why Jesus sometimes lets us live a while on our own. Even the feeling of being distant from him is all part of the experience of his love.

In the passage above, the disciples finally understand that Jesus is preparing them for his absence. Their hearts must have been breaking at the thought that their beloved Master was going away. But Jesus tells them, "Trust me." He may seem absent from them for a while, but he is preparing a place for them where they will ultimately live with him forever.

Today, while Jesus is getting your room ready so you can live with him forever, he's also getting your heart ready, shaping your life, helping you to become the person he created you to be. Perhaps he wants to grow you up in him, pushing and exploring your faith, your beliefs, your very life, so you learn how to live in the realm of his love, waiting for his return, but becoming more mature in the process.

Someday you will be together with him again. You will live where he lives. Fully, maturely, richly, forever.

❋ *Jesus, it is hard to wait. I want everything and I want it now. I want to be in your presence fully and continually. But I understand the process of growth and maturity. I look forward to the promise of eternal life with you. Help me in that process. Give me some understanding of what's going on, so I can continue on the path you've set for me and not give up, knowing you are waiting for me at the end. You're with me every step of the way.*

fifty-six

NEVER ALONE

> Jesus said, "I will not leave you orphaned. I'm coming back. In just a little while the world will no longer see me, but you're going to see me because I am alive and you're about to come alive. At that moment you will know absolutely that I'm in my Father, and you're in me, and I'm in you."
>
> (John 14:18–20)

Some time ago I saw the film *Finding Neverland,* based on incidents in the life of Sir James M. Barrie, who created *Peter Pan* and other children's classics. It was a magical retelling that provoked in me a sense—though I hate to admit it—of jealousy. Yes, Barrie, brilliantly portrayed by Johnny Depp, had some hardships in his life, but he seemed able always to connect to others out of a sense of genuine love. That life-giving connection revolutionized his life and led to great creativity and fulfillment.

Perhaps because of Barrie's sense of wonder and openness to others, his apparently natural ability to live in the experience of love, he seemed to make an unusual impact on people's lives—sometimes even without realizing it. When he joined the Athenaeum Club, the story goes, having never set foot in that exclusive London club before, he walked up to an elderly scientist and asked him politely to point him in the direction of the dining room. To Barrie's utter astonishment, the old man began crying, tears running down his ruddy, wrinkled face. The man told Barrie that he'd been a member of that club for five decades, and not once had anyone ever spoken to him.

Well, I've had lots of people talk to me in my five decades, but somehow I can identify with that old scientist. And then I hear Jesus speak to me, saying, "You are not alone."

You may feel as though you are. Your heart may seem an empty chasm, yearning to be filled. You may feel cut off from others, ignored, abandoned—an orphan, lost and forgotten. But you are never alone, because Jesus is with you. He is alive and living and working within you. What's more, he is coming back for you. You're going to see him, alive and living and working within you.

Everyone experiences periods of loneliness. We can be surrounded by people—even people who love us—and yet that sense of existential loneliness can persist at times. It feels as though we are the only person in the world suffering in just the way we are suffering. No one knows us, no one understands us.

When we're in that cold, dark place, it feels futile to reach out to those we trust for help and comfort. How will they respond? How can they understand? What if they reject us or are indifferent to our need?

But that is where faith comes in, faith that in the moment feels crushed by fear and abandonment. We can fan the flame of our flickering faith with simple prayer, opening our soul to the Spirit of renewal, opening our heart to the one who loves us and who understands us totally—Jesus. Abandoned, lost, rejected, he faced torture and death on the cross. But he emerged in resurrection glory and power, which means we can trust him when he says he's not going to abandon us and that he's coming back for us. We can trust that he's here with us, right now. We can trust that "you will know absolutely that I'm in my Father, and you're in me, and I'm in you." Forever.

❋ *Jesus, in those dark nights of my soul, help me to trust you, lean on you, knowing you are here. Always here. Forever and ever, here with me. Help me truly to believe that I am never alone. Fill me with your presence and use me to reach out to others who feel orphaned and alone.*

fifty-seven
NO GAMES

> Jesus said, "The person who knows my commandments and keeps them, that's who loves me. And the person who loves me will be loved by my Father, and I will love him and make myself plain to him."
>
> Judas (not Iscariot) said, "Master, why is it that you are about to make yourself plain to us but not to the world?"
>
> "Because a loveless world," said Jesus, "is a sightless world. If anyone loves me, he will carefully keep my word and my Father will love him—we'll move right into the neighborhood! Not loving me means not keeping my words. The message you are hearing isn't mine. It's the message of the Father who sent me." (John 14:21–24)

If you really loved me, you'd do this for me. Have you ever heard those words from a spouse or friend or parent? You probably have, maybe thousands of times. Guilt is a very effective motivator and such emotional manipulation often works.

When Jesus says, "If anyone loves me, he will carefully keep my word," is he trying to make us feel guilty? Not at all. He's simply stating reality. The natural result of loving him and following him is living as he lived, with compassion and love and purpose.

When we fall in love with Jesus, he makes clear his expectations: love me and love your neighbor as yourself. He doesn't beat around the bush or play manipulation games. There's no guessing about what he wants from us or how he feels about us at any given moment. But we live in a world filled with manipulation, a world blind to true love—sacrificial, servant-hearted love, the kind of love that Jesus demonstrated and shares with you, and desires from you. That's why at face value it may seem as though Jesus is being manipulative. We're so used to playing these games that we immediately assume our role in them.

But open your eyes. You are no longer part of the sightless world. You are loved by Jesus and by God the Father, and they have moved right into your heart to dwell with you as you live your life.

When you love Jesus fully and honestly, you will live a whole, loving, obedient life. Jesus doesn't love you because you live that way. He simply loves you—and his love empowers you to follow him in every part of your life.

You don't earn Jesus' love by your careful obedience; you already possess his love. So, enjoy it. Revel in it. And then live out of that love. Live loved, and spread it around.

✻ *Jesus, thank you for the grace of your love. Thank you for loving me totally, eternally. Thank you for making yourself plain to me, for living within me. I love you. Let me live out of that love—let me be a loving servant to a sightless world, so that some eyes might be opened to the truth and some hearts might be opened to your limitless love.*

fifty-eight

PARTING GIFT

Jesus said, "I'm telling you these things while I'm still living with you. The Friend, the Holy Spirit whom the Father will send at my request, will make everything plain to you. He will remind you of all the things I have told you. I'm leaving

> you well and whole. That's my parting gift to you. Peace. I don't leave you the way you're used to being left—feeling abandoned, bereft. So don't be upset. Don't be distraught."
>
> (John 14:25–27)

I admit I sometimes watch "Wheel of Fortune" and even fantasize about someday being one of the contestants. There's always an irritatingly brilliant champion who wins lots of cash and prizes (usually the winner insists on exuberantly high-fiving the losers, only adding to their shame). But the poor person who never got a right answer, never caught a good break only winds up with a few consolation bucks or a "lovely parting gift" and an embarrassed handshake before he or she is quickly hustled offstage. I often wonder what that parting gift might be and what the losing contestant might want to do with it.

This is not the case, however, with the parting gift Jesus leaves his disciples. He promises to give them something far better than the grand prize of any game show. He will leave them "well and whole." He will replace their distress with his peace. He will, in fact, send them a Friend, the Holy Spirit, to fill them and guide them and remind them of what Jesus taught them about living and loving as children of God.

And he promises to do the same for us.

If you identify with the emotions the disciples were experiencing—feeling abandoned, bereft, upset, and distraught—Jesus says he can give you peace, he can leave you "well and whole." Can you trust that? Do you believe it? Even when it doesn't feel true, can you rely on that word from your loving Master?

The Spirit within you can, even now, enable you to experience Jesus' love. He wants to open you up, make things plain to you, give you peace, and help you to overcome the emptiness and frustrations and setbacks you encounter in this world.

What will you do with Jesus' lovely parting gift to you? First you must accept it.

Then unwrap it.

Then put it to good use.

❋ *Jesus, I yearn for your peace. I am desperate for wholeness. I realize I am the only thing keeping me from experiencing those wonderful grace gifts from you to me through the Spirit. Help me to accept the gift you have given me. Help me to unwrap it and put it to good use today.*

fifty-nine

AT HOME WITH JESUS

> Jesus said, "I've loved you the way my Father has loved me. Make yourselves at home in my love. If you keep my commands, you'll remain intimately at home in my love. That's what I've done—kept my Father's commands and made myself at home in his love." (John 15:9–10)

Even in strange and unusual places, it's easy to feel at home if we are safe, welcomed, comfortable, and loved. I've felt at home in a number of places, even by myself in a cottage near the ocean, or at a house on a gorgeous North Georgia lake, or in a cabin surrounded by forested hills. But usually I feel most at home in the presence of family and friends.

I remember a couple of years ago nervously anticipating a trip home to see my parents and siblings. I hadn't seen my folks and my sister in West Virginia, several states away from me, in nearly six months, and it had been nearly two years since I had seen my two brothers. Much had happened in our lives since we had last been together, a lot of difficult situations to deal with all around. I felt some trepidation especially about seeing one of my brothers, who had some disagreements with me politically and theologically. We hadn't really even spoken in some time. But then, shortly before I left for the trip, I got a quick email from that brother expressing excitement about seeing me and signing off with "love."

As it turned out, my nervousness was unwarranted. We gathered together around some delicious meals and lots of conversation, much laughter and some serious discussion. Our preacher Dad prayed over our meals, or we sang a prayer of thanks as we often did at mealtimes when growing up. Despite the difficulties, the differences of opinion, the heartbreaks, the fears, we were family together, accepting and loving no matter what. We were home.

As it turned out, it would be one of the last times we were all together like that at our folks' home, as within half a year both Mom and Dad began experiencing major health issues simultaneously, eventually ending up in different care facilities. I'd drive home as often as I could, at least once a month or so, to visit my folks and whatever other sibling happened to be there at the same time. Each visit was a blessed reminder of the unshakable love of my family.

There is nothing like the feeling of feeling "at home." According to Jesus, we can feel this way anywhere if we acknowledge his presence, consciously living with him and realizing we are intimately at home in his love. We can feel at home even in the car stuck in traffic on the way to work, in the midst of frenetic activity at our house, or in our office as we answer ringing phones and inquisitive emails—and even while living in a house where tensions and fears tear at our faith or where an unexpected crisis shatters normality. Wherever we find ourselves, we can be present to God's love, making it possible for us to feel at home. It comes when we acknowledge the reality Jesus speaks of.

Jesus isn't saying, "Keep loving me." He is saying, "Keep knowing and possessing and enjoying and experiencing the love I have for you always." He carries the burden of loving us.

Listen to Jesus. You are his beloved. Just as the Father loves him—totally, completely, fully—so he loves you. But notice, being at home in his love requires some effort on our part: We must *make ourselves* at home in his love. Other translations say continue in, live in, remain faithful in, abide. All active verbs, not passive.

When I find myself feeling comforted and loved in a home or cabin or lake house, it reminds me that it's possible to make myself at home with Jesus, no matter where I am. Where do you experience this kind of all-is-wellness, this restorative peace, this rejuvenating comfort? Make yourself intimately at home with Jesus. He's waiting for you there—wherever it may be for you, even if it's right where you are right now.

❋ *Jesus, wherever I go, you are there, dwelling within me, beckoning me to come be with you, embracing me with your love and care. I want to spend some time with you and then go forth renewed and refreshed with a vision of how I can take your love to the world around me.*

sixty

RELENTLESS BECKONING

> Jesus said, "I still have many things to tell you, but you can't handle them now. But when the Friend comes, the Spirit of Truth, he will take you by the hand and guide you into all the truth there is. He won't draw attention to himself, but will make sense out of what is about to happen and, indeed, out of all that I have done and said. He will honor me; he will take from me and deliver it to you." (John 16:12–14)

Think back over your life. If you knew ten, twenty, thirty years ago what you know now, the problems you'd face with your family, your career, every aspect of your life, what would you have done? Would that knowledge have drawn you forward or would it have terrified you into retreat?

God knows exactly how much we need to know, and when. Thankfully, we only know what we need to know when we need to know it. Some things we simply aren't ready for yet.

My life has taken many twists and turns, and I look back with some shock at how things have shifted and changed and progressed in my faith, my career, my family, and my personal growth. I look back at my mistakes and the decisions I've made that ended up costing far more than I had anticipated. Yet I know God has been with me through all of it. I believe that my journey, with its starts and stops, its ups and downs, its steps forward and backward, has been part of God's work to make me whole and true. At times I have fought this growth process, to be sure. I have struggled with it, denied it, and ignored it. But God is always moving, relentlessly beckoning, lovingly coaxing me forward, closer to God's will for me. Closer to the image of Christ. Closer to love.

God's love calls us to live with greater awareness of Christ's presence with us, his calling on our lives, and his challenge to sacrifice for others. The Spirit helps us live loved:

- By helping us hear the voice of Jesus, learning what we need to learn just when we need to learn it.
- By showing us the wrong paths we take, guiding us back into the arms of our Savior when we stray.
- By giving us the strength and courage to take the bold steps we never, ever expected to have to take.
- By making some sense out of all the nonsense, all the tragedy, all the unexpected consequences, all the bad choices we make.
- By learning to accept those things that do not make sense as part of God's work in our lives and keep going.
- By releasing holy peace in our hearts as we surrender to moving in the current of the Savior's will for us, taking us wherever it will without our fighting it.

Because he loves us, God has given us the Spirit to help us to become the people God created us to be, to help us to become more loving as we grow in our awareness that we are Christ's beloved. Thank God we have a holy Friend to walk with, hand in hand, guiding us and loving us along the way into the truth.

Jesus, you know me so well. You know what I need when I need it. You have provided the sublime holy resource, the Friend, who guides me and teaches me along the way. How can I thank you?

sixty-one

THE ETERNAL NOW

Raising his eyes in prayer, Jesus said:
"Father, it's time.
Display the bright splendor of your Son
So the Son in turn may show your bright splendor.
You put him in charge of everything human
So he might give real and eternal life to all in his charge.
And this is the real and eternal life:
That they know you,
The one and only true God,
And Jesus Christ, whom you sent." (John 17:1–3)

When I was just out of college, I was going through a particularly rough time. I was alone in a new town, far away from home and family and friends, and trying to figure out a new job, cope with an eccentric boss, and learn a new way of life. It was a rough transition. I was starting over from scratch, building a new life. It was hard and lonely work.

One day I received a greeting card in the mail from a friend who knew that I had been down about all this. The front of the card said, "Keep looking down."

I reacted with a smirk. *I'm already looking down! That's my problem!* But then I opened the card. "Keep looking down . . . you are seated with Christ in the heavenlies."

According to Ephesians 2:6, that's the way Jesus looks at our lives. We're already with him in eternity. We are living above the counterfeit and have entered into the authentic. We are beyond the temporal and temporary and fleeting, and we are living in the eternal with the one who loves us so much he died for us.

Jesus knew his death was approaching. He knew the purpose of that death: to give "real and eternal" life to those who had entered into his circle of love. You are in that circle now. It is the circle of those who know God, the one and only true God, and the Son whom he sent. It is the circle of those who are living, right now, the "real and eternal life."

Realizing this can put your life into context. The fears, doubts, loneliness, and longings you may be feeling are not the ultimate reality. Yes, they're real. You feel them deeply. But they are temporary. They're not the whole story. The real and eternal life you've been given is happening right now.

Do you realize it? Can you see it?

❋ *Jesus, thank you for praying for me, for including me in the circle of your love. Help me to live eternally, consciously, knowing you are with me wherever I am and whatever is happening around me. I want to know you more and more.*

sixty-two

THE OBJECT OF PRAYER

Raising his eyes in prayer, Jesus said:
"I'm not asking that you take them out of the world
But that you guard them from the Evil One.
They are no more defined by the world
Than I am defined by the world.
Make them holy—consecrated—with the truth;
Your word is consecrating truth.
In the same way that you gave me a mission in the world,
I give them a mission in the world.
I'm consecrating myself for their sakes
So they'll be truth-consecrated in their mission."

(John 17:15–19)

Jesus didn't ask the Father to get us out of here. No, our loving Savior asked God to protect us from the Evil One while we are living in this world. Why?

- So God, rather than the selfish culture we're surrounded by, can build our character.
- So God can offer us the broad, wide sustenance of the Word through the Scriptures, rather than the shallow, simple musings of small-thinking humans.
- So God can heal our wounds, rather than our letting them fester with infection.
- So God can give us a calling, a mission, with meaning and purpose and value, rather than our following a personal whimsy or self-centered desire.
- So God can incite us to reach out and share holy love rather than keeping to our own silly interests.

Jesus is praying to the Father for you. He wants you protected, so you can be holy, consecrated—set apart with him and for him—and ready for whatever mission he's preparing you for.

How is the Father answering that prayer in your life today?

❋ *Jesus, you challenge me to seek your presence, your truth, your holiness, right now in the midst of the life I'm living. Prepare me in whatever ways you need for the mission you have called me to pursue. Thank you for trusting me with this.*

sixty-three

I AM

So Judas led the way to the garden, and the Roman soldiers and police sent by the high priests and Pharisees followed. They arrived there with lanterns and torches and swords. Jesus, knowing by now everything that was coming down on him, went out and met them. He said, "Who are you after?"

They answered, "Jesus the Nazarene."

He said, "That's me." The soldiers recoiled, totally taken aback. (John 18:3–5)

Jesus knew what was happening that night. He saw Judas. He saw the soldiers and their weapons and the fierce looks on their faces. He knew his destiny. Still, he asks them—forces them—to clearly state their purpose: "Who are you after?"

They responded in the clipped manner of soldiers on a mission: "Jesus the Nazarene."

Jesus answered them simply, "That's me," and the soldiers and officials fell backward in shock. Jesus' words stunned them; the original Greek indicates he had simply said, "I am."

- Were they so amazed by his direct admission that they recoiled in surprise?
- Were they shocked that this Jesus would so blasphemously use precisely the same self-identifying words God had used at Mount Sinai?
- Were they stunned to realize that they were merely actors on an infinite, eternal stage and that their actions would set into motion a revolutionary change in human history, and human lives, forever?

Imagine that you are John, the beloved disciple. You've been praying with Jesus in the olive grove. You've experienced his loving companionship. You've witnessed the approaching mob. You've heard Jesus reveal himself. Do you fall down? Do you know what's happening? Do you realize where this is all leading?

His words ring in your ears: "I am." Present tense. Jesus is still with us, in the present tense. He is still God with us. And his love will lead us into the eternal presence of the Father.

The next time a worldly mob, an unexpected attack, or an apparent personal reversal confronts you, remember that.

Jesus, I know the rest of this story and yet I still shake my head in fear and confusion and disbelief. Help me to hear your "I am" through the day, to remember who you are and what you did for me, to help me to realize you are always here, to remind me that you are God with me.

sixty-four

KING OF HEARTS

"My kingdom," said Jesus, "doesn't consist of what you see around you. If it did, my followers would fight so that I wouldn't be handed over to the Jews. But I'm not that kind of king, not the world's kind of king."

Then Pilate said, "So, are you a king or not?"

Jesus answered, "You tell me. Because I am King, I was born and entered the world so that I could witness to the truth. Everyone who cares for truth, who has any feeling for the truth, recognizes my voice."

Pilate said, "What is truth?" (John 18:36–38)

I remember two times in my life when I heard Jesus' voice, almost audibly.

The first came many years ago. I was so tied up in fear about losing an important friendship that I was helping to cause its destruction. As I sat one morning in my easy chair, stewing about it all, out of the blue I heard the words, "Let go of the fear and the love will remain."

The message shocked me with its clarity, its rightness. Since that time I have tried to remember those words whenever I find myself getting anxious or fearful about an important relationship, and I've found that when I let go of the self-centered fears, the love remains and grows.

The words were true, and I recognized the voice.

The second time was more recent, as I struggled over an internal issue. I lay in bed early one morning, chastising myself, judging myself, angry with myself. Another word came to me, clear and light: "Stop hating yourself."

The words surprised me—they seemed to come out of nowhere. Initially, I got defensive. *I don't hate myself! That's silly!* But slowly it dawned on me that that was exactly what I was doing and that self-hatred was only hurting me and keeping me from dealing with the longstanding struggle in positive, healthy ways.

The words were true, and I recognized the voice.

Jesus came to tell the truth, and only those who are predisposed to hear the truth can hear his voice. Only those who are willing to hear the truth, accept it, live it out—regardless of the pain and sacrifice and hard work involved—can recognize Jesus' voice, the voice of truth, the voice of love.

Do you want to know the truth? If so, you'll recognize Jesus' voice when he speaks to you. You'll hear the promptings, the comfort, the challenges, the reassurances. You'll hear the calling, the mission he has for you. You'll hear the areas of your life that need the Spirit's attention and your surrender.

You'll know the truth—and you'll recognize the voice.

❋ *Jesus, I think I keep my spiritual ears plugged up sometimes—my own internal babble shuts you out. I want to know the truth. Speak to me. Thank you for loving me enough to do that.*

sixty-five

EVEN BETTER BLESSINGS

Eight days later, his disciples were again in the room. This time Thomas was with them. Jesus came through the locked doors, stood among them, and said, "Peace to you."

Then he focused his attention on Thomas. "Take your finger and examine my hands. Take your hand and stick it in my side. Don't be unbelieving. Believe."

Thomas said, "My Master! My God!"

Jesus said, "So, you believe because you've seen with your own eyes. Even better blessings are in store for those who believe without seeing." (John 20:26–29)

Recently I heard Barbara Lundblad describe this story as the most intimate in all the Bible: Thomas placing his hand inside the breast wound of his loving Lord. Thomas had wanted proof, and Jesus was giving it to him—physically.

Do you sometimes feel a lot like this doubting Thomas, *wanting* proof?

Thomas got his proof in the form of the wounds in the hands and side of Jesus' resurrected body—the Word made flesh. Humbled and overwhelmed, Thomas proclaimed Jesus his Master, his God.

Jesus gently chided his friend and brother, and in so doing he blesses you and me. We have not been given the opportunity that Thomas had, to actually see Jesus physically, to touch him, to feel the wounds that proved his mastery over death. Yet we believe without seeing—and so we are blessed "even better."

That's a good word to remember when your faith falters, the light dims, and the darkness of doubt intrudes.

- When you must deal with unexpected news from your doctor.
- When you are faced with a difficult challenge with your child.
- When your financial resources seem so woefully inadequate for your needs.
- When your job feels like a dead end, a waste of time.
- When you face a major disagreement with your spouse that seems insurmountable.
- When a lifelong dream fades away.
- When a loved one dies.

Better blessings are in store for you. In responding to God positively you will experience his love in this life. When you know you are loved by the God-man who overcame death, who is with you wherever you are, you will see and experience blessings you never saw—and probably doubted—before.

Some months ago Pastor Bradley Schmeling recorded a sermon for the *Day1* radio program, and in it he quoted his favorite prayer:

> Lord God, you have called your servants to ventures of which we cannot see the ending, by paths as yet untrodden, through perils unknown. Give us faith to go out with good courage, not knowing where we go, but only that your hand is leading us and your love supporting us; through Jesus Christ our Lord.[17]

If we truly pray that prayer, there is little room for doubt. Jesus says to you, "Don't be unbelieving. Believe."

❋ *Jesus, I acknowledge that sometimes I feel a lot like Thomas. Thank you that you trust me with doubts and darkness, because those things can teach me to trust you even more. Thank you for the blessings of believing you and trusting your love.*

Part Three

SHARING HIS LOVE

sixty-six
FIRST STEPS

> Three days later there was a wedding in the village of Cana in Galilee. Jesus' mother was there. Jesus and his disciples were guests also. When they started running low on wine at the wedding banquet, Jesus' mother told him, "They're just about out of wine."
>
> Jesus said, "Is that any of our business, Mother—yours or mine? This isn't my time. Don't push me." (John 2:1–4)

Mary knew. She had lived with Jesus for over three decades. She'd given birth to him, raised him, and guided him as all good mothers do. She knew he could fix the slightly embarrassing situation. Mary knew he could make it right. But Jesus was at the brink of a ministry that would last only a few short years, a ministry people still talk about two thousand years later. Every day. Everywhere.

Jesus knew his mother and her ways, typical of many mothers. Just a nudge, a suggestion, a wink, and you know what they want. You can almost sense the exasperation in Jesus' voice. "This isn't our problem," he says. "This isn't my time."

Was he hesitant to step forward as someone special, someone God had sent to share his love? Was that why Jesus said, "This isn't my time"? After all, he was at a party. He had just gathered his disciples, those who would live with him, follow him, be with him, preparing for the next step. He'd come to honor the occasion of marriage. He'd come to have fun with friends. Now this.

It doesn't seem as though Mary paid much attention to his refusal. The next moment she's instructing the servants: "Whatever he tells you, do it" (2:5). Before you know it, Jesus has performed his first public miracle, changing huge earthenware jugs of water into carafes of fine wine.

Mary knew what Jesus could do. She knew her son. She knew what he had come to do. And clearly, so did Jesus. He was ready to unleash God's miraculous love on a world that needed it. He was ready to share a new way of life that would change the rules, even the rules of physics and medicine and theology and all of life.

He was ready to pour the wine of divine love into the world. And into you. His loving acts reverberate through history and land right in your heart. But they're not meant to stay there. You have to take a step out to share God's love with others.

❋ *Jesus, I don't know if I'm ready to take that first step on a journey of sharing your love wholeheartedly—a journey that may lead somewhere difficult or frightening, that may totally change the life I know now and am so comfortable with. But you were ready. And I am with you. And somehow, that makes me feel safe. Wherever I go, to wedding feasts and soup kitchens, in joyous times and hard times, you are with me. Help me to take that first step of obedience to God's will, to reach out in love—no matter where I think it will lead me.*

sixty-seven

AGENDA OF LOVE

Jesus explained, "I'm not interested in crowd approval. And do you know why? Because I know you and your crowds. I know that love, especially God's love, is not on your working agenda. I came with the authority of my Father, and you either dismiss me or avoid me. If another came, acting self-important, you would welcome him with open arms. How do you expect to get anywhere with God when you spend all your time jockeying for position with each other, ranking your rivals and ignoring God?" (John 5:41–44)

We can read Jesus' caustic blast against the self-important religious leaders of Israel and cheer him on. "You tell 'em, Jesus!" But we should take time to let his words address our hearts too, because we, like those religious leaders, can so easily get off track, thinking we have everything figured out in our faith and life—and not leaving any room for Jesus in it.

So, take some time to ask yourself some questions the religious leaders should have asked themselves. Am I too busy

- just getting along?
- seeking approval?
- getting noticed?
- working to be liked?
- trying not to make waves?

Am I caught up in

- comparing myself with others?
- seeking to use others to better myself?
- building rivalries and competitions to get ahead?
- assuming I have all the right answers?
- acting self-important?

Or is sharing love—especially God's love—on my agenda today? If so, if love were to saturate the schedule I've digitally encoded on my PDA or typed in my computer or scrawled in my Day-Timer, what would it look like?

Jesus does not hint. He does not passively hope that you will hear him, let him in, let him love you, let him love others through you. He challenges you. He boldly and clearly lets you know what he wants.

Then he leaves it up to you as to how you will respond.

Jesus, you are asking me to take a hard look at how I interact with others—and with you. You are asking me to do radical things to my schedule, my purpose, my way of living, my relationships. You are demanding, lovingly but strongly, to be my Lord. I am ready to respond.

sixty-eight
RADICAL OBEDIENCE

Jesus said, "Don't be nitpickers; use your head—and heart!—to discern what is right, to test what is authentically right."
(John 7:24)

The religious leaders were angry with Jesus for breaking the Sabbath law. He had dared to heal a man on the day God set aside for rest. Rather than seeing the miracle, this explosion of God's powerful grace and transformation in a human life, they saw only the law Jesus had ignored for the greater good. Jesus begs them to rethink their priorities, but it is a lost cause.

I couldn't help but think of this story when, some months ago, I heard the testimony of a minister who clearly loved Jesus and desired to be his ambassador. In the days following September 11, 2001, this person participated in an interfaith gathering to offer consolation and hope to the grieving people of New York City, as well as to the whole nation. He offered a moving prayer at the end of the service, which was attended by representatives of a wide range of denominations and religions. However, his denomination forbade public prayer offered in the presence of non-Christians. He had broken a rule of his church.

Despite the fact that he had been given permission—twice—by the head of the denomination to participate in the service, a number of people called for his dismissal. For more than two years he was forced to appear before church committees and denominational courts to answer for his lawbreaking. All because he wanted to share the love of Christ and the comfort of God's presence to all in the midst of profound grief.

Are you holding on to some rules, even very good ones, so tightly that you can't "use your head—and your heart!—to discern what is right, to test what is authentically right"? If so, open your hand and let the rule go. Rules are made to provide some structure and protection in our life. But sometimes rules can be broken for the greater good.

When the Spirit moves us to reach out in risky ways, even if a rule must be broken, our love for God demands our obedience. Such obedience gives life.

❋ *Jesus, I want to do what is right in your eyes, even when it risks a reaction from close-minded people. I want to respond to your Spirit today in healing, loving ways. I want to use my head and my heart to serve you, no matter the cost.*

sixty-nine

ENERGETICALLY AT WORK

> His disciples asked, "Rabbi, who sinned: this man or his parents, causing him to be born blind?"
>
> Jesus said, "You're asking the wrong question. You're looking for someone to blame. There is no such cause-effect here. Look instead for what God can do. We need to be energetically at work for the One who sent me here, working while the sun shines. When night falls, the workday is over. For as long as I am in the world, there is plenty of light. I am the world's Light." (John 9:2–5)

When something goes wrong, when someone is hurt, when a mistake happens, the first question we ask is often, "Whose fault is this?" We want justice. We want the comfort of seeing a cause-and-effect that makes sense, that seems fair. We want heads to roll!

The disciples assumed someone had to be at fault to cause the poor man they passed by to be blind. It had to be either his fault or his parents'. But Jesus claims the question of blame is wrong-headed. Instead, Jesus says, look to the one who can do something about it. Work through it. Transform people because of it. Instead of looking backward, look forward.

That's so hard to do. It's counterintuitive. But it's the way of Jesus. It's the way of love. Sure, somebody may be blameworthy, but Jesus calls us to look beyond the fault and see the need—and be an instrument of God's healing for that need.

Instead of spending our time and energy finding fault, "we need to be energetically at work" for God. We need to be vessels for God's grace and love and healing touch, just as Jesus was with this blind man. That means being willing to sacrifice some time, energy, and comfort to listen and serve and love others. We need to be reflectors of the light of Jesus into the darkness of life's pain and tragedy. We need to work while the sun shines, trusting the Son to give us the wisdom and love to provide God's solutions instead of asking useless questions.

We need to be available to do that today.

❋ *Jesus, I confess I do get caught up in useless pursuits that keep me from being available to work energetically for you, sharing your love with others who need it so badly. Keep me aware of this tendency, so I can overcome it in your power. I want to be a channel for your loving presence today.*

seventy

INTO THE CLEAR LIGHT

> Jesus then said, "I came into the world to bring everything into the clear light of day, making all the distinctions clear, so that those who have never seen will see, and those who have made a great pretense of seeing will be exposed as blind."
>
> (John 9:39)

When Jesus walked the earth, he shined the light of God's love, truth, and grace on every situation he faced, and he calls us to follow his example. Those who thought they could see were revealed to be blind and those who had never been able to see the truth had it brought in focus.

This is what Jesus does:

- He shatters assumptions.
- He causes havoc among those who feel safe and secure in their own little worlds.
- He shakes the foundations on which we have carefully constructed our faulty beliefs and selfish practices.
- He strips away wrongly placed pride and self-importance.
- He raises what has been downtrodden, abused, and ignored.
- He shines the clear, bright light of God's love and truth into every dark, fetid corner of human existence.

That's what he did when he walked this earth, and he's still doing these things.

Yet sometimes we approach Jesus as though he were merely a character in an ancient book who had some interesting things to say about life and God. We see him as someone whose purpose is to give us comfort and solace and good feelings, regardless of how we're living our lives. We see him as patting us on the back for our pleasant lives, our safe beliefs, our not causing any problems in the world.

Do you sense the disconnect in your life as deeply as I do? Does this picture of Jesus as one who turns the world on its head conflict with how you want him to work in your life—safely, at your beck and call, simply for moral support?

If Jesus were to stand before you and the clear light of his loving will spilled all over you and poured deeply into your heart, what do you think your life would look like as a result? Would you suddenly find yourself blind? Or would you finally be able to see?

Jesus, I know you love me, because you care enough to challenge me so, to help me to know myself, be myself, as you have called me to be. Shine the light of clarity on my presuppositions, my expectations, my assumptions, so I can see them for what they are. Open my eyes to your way. If that means turning my world upside down, so be it.

seventy-one

ONE GLORIOUS FLOCK

> Jesus said, "I am the Good Shepherd. I know my own sheep and my own sheep know me. In the same way, the Father knows me and I know the Father. I put the sheep before myself, sacrificing myself if necessary. You need to know that I have other sheep in addition to those in this pen. I need to gather and bring them, too. They'll also recognize my voice. Then it will be one flock, one Shepherd." (John 10:14–16)

As Jesus describes his work and ministry to the antagonistic religious leaders, he reveals something that shocks them: He not only is the good Shepherd to those who know him, the Jews, but he has other sheep he intends to gather and bring into the pen of God's eternal love and care.

Jesus is the good Shepherd to the world. Those who are his—no matter where they are or when they live—will also recognize his voice. They will all belong to one glorious flock, following one amazing Shepherd. But when Jesus told the religious leaders this, they became outraged. The Israelites believed that God was *their* God. Other nations, other peoples—they could have their own gods; they could fend for themselves. Even those who followed Jesus considered him to be *their* Messiah, just for Israel—their long-awaited king.

I wonder how we would have reacted if we had heard from this man that God's love was for far more than just the "family"? That the good Shepherd had come not just for us and our people, but for everyone?

Even more important, how would we react if we truly heard that news now? How uncomfortable would we be if we understood that Jesus' love and care extends to people very different from us—different skin colors or lifestyles or economic levels or social situations?

God's love encompasses the whole, wide world. Look around you in your sheep pen. Your work. Your neighborhood. Your church. Your circle of friends. Your life in every aspect. Is Jesus telling you, "I have other sheep in addition to those in this pen. I need to gather and bring them in too, and I need you to help"?

Jesus has accepted you in love. You can do the same for others, whoever they may be. It's all part of living loved.

❋ *Jesus, my circles are admittedly small. Open my heart to the whole world. Help me to stretch out of my own comfort zone, to reach out and welcome others who are different from me, but who are all part of the same flock, all following the same loving Shepherd.*

seventy-two

FRAGRANT SACRIFICE

> Mary came in with a jar of very expensive aromatic oils, anointed and massaged Jesus' feet, and then wiped them with her hair. The fragrance of the oils filled the house.
>
> Judas Iscariot, one of his disciples, even then getting ready to betray him, said, "Why wasn't this oil sold and the money given to the poor? It would have easily brought three hundred silver pieces." . . .
>
> Jesus said, "Let her alone. She's anticipating and honoring the day of my burial. You always have the poor with you. You don't always have me." (John 12:3–8)

Jesus and his closest friends—his disciples, Lazarus, Mary, and Martha—gathered for dinner. There was likely some small talk and joking, some serious discussion of the day's events, and a lot of asking Lazarus how he was feeling, since he'd just been raised from the dead.

While Martha worked in the kitchen and served supper, Mary did something surprising, something very selfless, and yet intimate and loving. She anointed Jesus' feet with expensive oil, massaged them, and wiped them with her long hair. She sacrificially expressed her thanks for the love she experienced from her Master.

As the fragrance hung in the air, no doubt so did many emotions. Mary's outrageous behavior surely shocked many of the disciples. Martha was likely angry with her sister for drawing the focus onto herself while Martha slaved away in the kitchen. Judas was outraged at the money wasted in this silly act. But Mary's selfless, loving gesture deeply moved Jesus. It demonstrated to him that she understood what lay ahead for him. It was an act of worship and adoration for the one who would not be with his beloved friends much longer.

It's a moving story, rich with emotion and sensuality. Can you put yourself into the cast?

- *You are one of the shocked disciples,* who can't seem to look beyond the surface act to the meaning behind it, the true love and worship it communicated to Jesus.
- *You are Judas,* who may have his mind already made up that Jesus is not the answer, but who nevertheless gets so caught up in the nuts and bolts of life and finances and realities that he can't stand the wastefulness.
- *You are Martha,* who is toiling away to serve everyone, feeling hurt and jealous of her sister, who gets all the attention from Jesus while Martha's left with the dirty dishes.
- *You are Mary,* who sacrificially gives to the Lord she loves not only expensive oil, but also her care, her tears, her love, and her dignity.

Who do you identify with most? What will it take to move your mindset into one of willingness to sacrificially share and serve?

Jesus, life has so many levels of understanding. Help me to look beyond the surface reality—to which I often overreact—and see the deeper truth beneath it. Help me to take advantage of opportunities to love and serve you sacrificially in ways I may have never considered before. And to follow through with no thought of the reactions of others around me, because I love you.

seventy-three
LOVING RECKLESSLY

> Jesus answered, "Listen carefully: Unless a grain of wheat is buried in the ground, dead to the world, it is never any more than a grain of wheat. But if it is buried, it sprouts and reproduces itself many times over. In the same way, anyone who holds on to life just as it is destroys that life. But if you let it go, reckless in your love, you'll have it forever, real and eternal." (John 12:24–25)

Bury a grain of wheat in the ground and it grows and brings forth something wonderful and new and alive. Bury the Savior in a tomb, and he is resurrected to glory and power, enabling all who follow to experience something wonderful and new and alive.

In the same way, if you let your life loose in the power of the Spirit, if you live recklessly in your love for God, then you will experience a life worth living.

Mary exhibited reckless love when she sacrificed her modesty and her valuable perfume in loving service to her Lord, massaging his feet with costly perfumed oil and wiping them with her hair. You could demonstrate reckless love by sacrificially giving or serving the lowest and the least in your community, or in your world. Or by forgiving someone who needs your love, even though you know you're right. Or by accepting an unexpected ministry opportunity even though it doesn't fit into your safe plans.

- What grain of wheat are you holding on to, not allowing to "die" in the ground to bring forth something new and glorious?
- What part of your life are you trying to protect, to keep "alive," not realizing that you are actually stifling your life and keeping it from being what God created it to be?

- What part of your life or love are you keeping boxed up, tamped down, for fear of letting go and getting hurt?

I came across a quotation from Henri Nouwen that I think captures the essence of these verses:

> Do not hesitate to love and to love deeply. The more you have loved and have allowed yourself to suffer because of your love, the more you will be able to let your heart grow wider and deeper.[18]

Jesus says, let go. Let the grain of wheat die. Let your life die. Let your hesitancy, your resistance to love fully and recklessly die. And discover what it means to truly experience Jesus' love.

Jesus, I acknowledge my fear of life and love. That fear is keeping me from experiencing the life and love you want for me. I do want to let go of those fears and be transformed by your living presence, your energizing love. I want to live a "real and eternal" life.

seventy-four

WANTING TO SERVE

> Jesus answered, "If any of you want to serve me, then follow me. Then you'll be where I am, ready to serve at a moment's notice. The Father will honor and reward anyone who serves me." (John 12:26)

Follow me. Jesus summarizes the entire Christian experience in these words. Yet many of us keep putting it backward. We want to know:

- What's in it for me?
- How can I benefit? How can I profit?
- Who can help me get where I want to go? Who can I use to get my way?
- How can I manipulate or maneuver to get ahead?
- How can I get people to follow me?

Often we hide these questions beneath layers of rationalization. After all, it's the American way to succeed, to get ahead, to lead the pack. The American dream involves possessions, power, influence, money—and the personal sense of fulfillment those earthly things presumably bring. Many of us, whether in the United States or anywhere in the world, are willing to do whatever it takes to make that dream come true.

But Jesus starts from the opposite end of the spectrum. For him, it's not about acquiring, leading, or being served. It's all about serving him. But before we can serve him we have to *want* to serve him. That's the beginning point of ultimate fulfillment.

Do you want to serve Jesus? To serve others in Jesus' name and in Jesus' love? Does that yearning drive your thoughts and actions? Does that desire fuel your life? Once you can answer those questions with a fervent yes, then the rest falls right into place.

If you want to serve Jesus, then follow him. Follow him—into the dark places of the world that hunger for light, into the desperate needs of the human heart that cry out for love, into the pain and illness and loss that need the comforting presence of Christ.

When you follow him, you will be with him in his loving, empowering presence. You'll be ready to serve at a moment's notice, with a heart that's sensitive to the Spirit's moving. That is the way to live as a lover of Christ, to live as Christ's beloved.

By the way, that is also the way to ultimately experience the most amazing and fulfilling rewards and honors in life—not the ones the world clamors for, but the rewards and honors that come directly from the Father's hand.

❋ *Jesus, you make it sound so simple. "If, then." But that "if" seems like a huge mountain I have to cross. Work on my heart today. Build within me the desire to serve you, to follow you, to be ready to reach out in ways you would direct me.*

seventy-five

A PATTERN OF LOVE

After Jesus had finished washing their feet, he took his robe, put it back on, and went back to his place at the table.

Then he said, "Do you understand what I have done to you? You address me as 'Teacher' and 'Master,' and rightly so. That is what I am. So if I, the Master and Teacher, washed your feet, you must now wash each other's feet. I've laid down a pattern for you. What I've done, you do. I'm only pointing out the obvious. A servant is not ranked above his master; an employee doesn't give orders to the employer. If you understand what I'm telling you, act like it—and live a blessed life." (John 13:12–17)

Jesus, the Master and Teacher, assumed the role of the servant. He leads by serving in love, and he tells his followers to do the same.

Yet many Christians are building empires, living as though they deserve only the best, seeking fame and fortune through a sensational and self-promoting "ministry." This mentality is hardly restricted to the Christian church and organizational leaders. It trickles down to their followers, who seek God's blessings and prosperity and "abundance," which they define as tangible and financial rather than eternal and spiritual.

Jesus turns this attitude downside up. The God-man stripped down and washed dirty feet.

Think of those who have touched your life the most deeply. Weren't their actions marked by humility, simplicity, service, and love? I think of the woman—elderly but full of life and love—who taught me in vacation Bible school one summer and who challenged me to a life of creative service. I think of the pastor who took me under his wing when I was in college and, with his example of loving spiritual service, set a pattern for me to aspire to. I think of a minister who despite his confessed introversion was always willing to do whatever it took to be with people in times of difficulty or need to provide comfort, hope, and love. I think of so many who have touched my life with their mercy, wisdom, and love.

Who do you think of?

Humility, it's often said, is one of the most difficult character traits to possess, because once you think you have it, you've lost it. So, don't assume you have ever reached it. But certainly do all you can to serve others humbly, sacrificially, and lovingly. That's what Jesus did.

Today he says to you, "If you understand what I'm telling you, act like it—and live a blessed life."

❋ *Jesus, you have given me a pattern that is not easy to follow in this culture. But you have also given me many examples of men and women who have accepted your challenge to be a servant leader and to turn their world downside up in the process. Today I want to follow their loving example—and yours—through humble service. What opportunities will you give me to do that?*

seventy-six

NO STOPPING US

> Jesus said, "Let me give you a new command: Love one another. In the same way I loved you, you love one another. This is how everyone will recognize that you are my disciples—when they see the love you have for each other."
>
> (John 13:34–35)

When the world looks at your church, what do they see? Do they see a family loving one another, serving one another, learning from one another, challenging and encouraging one another, and welcoming all who would wish to attend? Or do they see a group of people fighting over who should be in charge, getting feelings hurt, failing to deal with essential issues, getting sidetracked on minor squabbles, and ignoring the rest of the world? Is that the way it's supposed to be? I wonder what Jesus would say.

Maybe he already said it: "Love one another." If we want to serve, this is what we must do: love. Those who follow Jesus are to follow his example and to love in the same ways he loved the twelve by

- teaching and healing them.
- being present to others.
- being utterly honest and guileless.
- expressing his—and our—truest, deepest feelings.
- serving others humbly.

Jesus says that when the world sees the love we have for one another in the community of faith, they will know that we are disciples of Jesus. This isn't to say we won't ever disagree with other believers but that we should work out any disagreements in an atmosphere of acceptance and understanding.

The disciples certainly were a mixed assortment of personalities, interests, and styles, yet Jesus was able to work with them and to give them this challenge, a challenge that stands for us today. It goes to the core of who we are as followers of Christ, as those he loves. It shows us that if we have trouble loving others in the body of Christ, perhaps we have not fully encountered and received and experienced the love Jesus has for us. As we've seen, this challenge starts with knowing about his love, then experiencing it, and then sharing it.

Once we've rested in the arms of our Master, once we've accepted our place as his beloved, nothing can stop us from loving others. If we want to.

Jesus, this is a challenging commandment you've given your disciples. Sometimes it is very hard to practice. I realize it starts with my accepting the love you have for me. I cannot love others out of my own resources—only yours. So, I call on those resources today. Help me to live out of this new commandment, and show the world how amazing your love for us is.

seventy-seven

EVEN GREATER THINGS

> Jesus said, "Believe me: I am in my Father and my Father is in me. If you can't believe that, believe what you see—these works. The person who trusts me will not only do what I'm doing but even greater things, because I, on my way to the Father, am giving you the same work to do that I've been doing. You can count on it. From now on, whatever you request along the lines of who I am and what I am doing, I'll do it. That's how the Father will be seen for who he is in the Son. I mean it. Whatever you request in this way, I'll do."
>
> (John 14:11–14)

The disciples were simple people. They were ordinary folks who worked for a living, paid bills, and had to fulfill all the mundane responsibilities of life. Some were married and had to take care of those relationships properly. A few certainly must have had children. They had all the ingredients for the recipe of ordinary, everyday people.

Just like us.

The disciples weren't anything special. They hadn't established themselves as prominent authorities in any field. They hadn't made a name for themselves. They possessed no special talent, no unusual gift for anything other than just living a regular life.

Just like us.

But Jesus called them. He called them to follow him, to be with him and learn from him. He called them to see him heal and touch and transform people's lives and to hear him teach amazingly simple yet startlingly counterintuitive truths.

Just as he has called us.

So, the disciples followed him, and they were amazed to see Jesus' astonishing works, to hear his challenging words. They'd never seen anyone do things like this. But Jesus told them that they would not only do the same work he did, but "even greater things."

Greater things than Jesus did? It's hard to believe. Yet Jesus really only touched the lives of a handful of people in a very small area of the planet. The disciples who followed him, and those who followed them even until today, have made an impact on the entire world, sharing the message of God's loving forgiveness and gracious acceptance in word and deed. As a result of their simple acts of obedience, the world is a different place.

Clearly those simple, ordinary men would become extraordinary servants in their work of spreading the good news about their Master. Many traveled far, worked hard, and ultimately gave their lives for the cause, just as their Master had done.

Jesus' words are meant for us too. He challenges us to follow him, to do even greater things for him. It's not about who we are—our personality or gifts or background. It's about how willing we are. How touched we are by Jesus' love. How filled we are by his Spirit.

So, what's stopping you? Even greater things await you.

❋ *Jesus, you are a tough act to follow. But clearly, your disciples took your words to heart and, in the power of the Spirit, did amazing things in your name and for God's glory. I want to be part of that. Please use me today to show people the love you have for them.*

seventy-eight

ANOTHER FRIEND

Jesus said, "If you love me, show it by doing what I've told you. I will talk to the Father, and he'll provide you another Friend so that you will always have someone with you. This Friend is the Spirit of Truth. The godless world can't take him in because it doesn't have eyes to see him, doesn't know what to look for. But you know him already because he has been staying with you, and will even be *in* you!" (John 14:15–17)

Think about these words from your Master—and notice that the starting point is your love for Jesus.

If you love me, he says, you will do something and I will do something. You will do what I have set out for you to do: Love one another. Serve others humbly. Reach out to those in need. Be an agent of healing and life.

And, if you love me, I will provide you with another Friend. I will not be with you in the flesh, but Someone will be with you always: the Spirit of Truth.

That's quite a love gift.

So often we leave a token of our love for someone when we have to be away from them—a card, a stuffed animal, a piece of jewelry or a book that means something to us. I still have Taffy, the stuffed toy dog my parents gave me when I was five years old and had to stay alone in a children's hospital—something to hug in their absence.

But Jesus gives us something beyond our wildest imaginings: He gives us the very presence of God in the form of the Spirit. As a child of God and lover of Jesus, you have God's Spirit with you, within you, and around you at all times.

You can't see him. The world certainly is unable to see him. But you can know the Spirit is with you and in you, holding you up, giving you strength, showing you the road ahead, filling you with peace and purpose and love. The Spirit helps you do what Jesus has told you to do, to share and to serve. You aren't on your own. You have a constant companion, a Friend to help you and guide you.

You can plumb the depths of even the simplest pronouncements of Jesus about the love relationship you share with him and still feel as though you never touch bottom. Understanding it—living it—requires a lifetime. But it all starts with your love for Jesus. And it will never end.

❋ *Jesus, I do love you. I am amazed by your love for me. I am challenged by your call to do your will. But I am blessed and empowered by the constant presence of the Spirit with me and in me. Thank you for loving and caring for me in this way.*

seventy-nine
ORGANIC LOVE

Jesus said, "I am the Real Vine and my Father is the Farmer. He cuts off every branch of me that doesn't bear grapes. And every branch that is grape-bearing he prunes back so it will bear even more. You are already pruned back by the message I have spoken.

"Live in me. Make your home in me just as I do in you. In the same way that a branch can't bear grapes by itself but only by being joined to the vine, you can't bear fruit unless you are joined with me.

"I am the Vine, you are the branches. When you're joined with me and I with you, the relation intimate and organic, the harvest is sure to be abundant. Separated, you can't produce a thing. Anyone who separates from me is deadwood, gathered up and thrown on the bonfire. But if you make yourselves at home with me and my words are at home in you, you can be sure that whatever you ask will be listened to and acted upon. This is how my Father shows who he is—when you produce grapes, when you mature as my disciples."

(John 15:1–8)

A few years ago, I planted English ivy in front of our house. A small rise had originally been reserved for an area of azalea bushes, but over the years several of them had died and the little hillside looked a bit unkempt and scraggly. A bed of ivy would look good there and would be relatively easy to maintain. So, I dug up all the old, brittle azalea plants that remained and prepared the ground. Then I purchased dozens of little plastic containers, each one holding a sprig of ivy. Those were planted a few feet apart from each other. After all this work, the little hillside still looked pretty pathetic. All you saw was an occasional sprig of ivy and a lot of plain old dirt.

After a couple of years, though, the ivy did its work. It spread across that little hillside area, intermingling, filling up all the empty spaces, producing thick greenery that looks just right. But now it must be kept in check; the ends of the vines have to be continually trimmed or they will grow right across the side-walk, up the tree adjacent to the bed, climbing the sides of the house.

I think of that ivy when I think of this passage. Jesus has set into motion something organic, something growing wildly, reaching out. This is the work of the body of Christ in the world—spreading, producing, filling, and covering. But unlike English ivy, this vine produces fruit, an abundant harvest of grapes. All this comes out of one Vine—Christ himself.

You are part of this fruitful vine. You are designed to become a growing, productive branch. You are joined with Jesus, and Jesus is joined with you. It is who you are as one of the beloved.

But there is a note of warning in Christ's words. Being part of the Vine, part of the outreach of God's love in the world, involves producing grapes. If a branch is not productive, it is removed. But, Jesus says, if you're joined with him, productivity should not be a problem. It's a natural flow from him through you to the world. Fruit results in abundance. It can't be stopped. It's like kudzu in the Southern countryside.

So, live in Jesus. "Make your home in me just as I do you." Experience the holy, intimate, organic relationship of love, and watch what happens through you as you share his love with the world around you.

❋ *Jesus, it all starts with the genuineness, the depth, of my relationship with you. If it is real and true and vital to me, all is well. Much fruit will result. So, help me to examine the fruit of my life—is it healthy? Abundant? And what does that tell me about the intimacy of my relationship with you?*

eighty

LIFE ON THE LINE

Jesus said, "I've told you these things for a purpose: that my joy might be your joy, and your joy wholly mature. This is my command: Love one another the way I loved you. This is the very best way to love. Put your life on the line for your friends." (John 15:11–13)

What have you done for love? Maybe you moved to a different city to be with the one you love. I just read a newspaper article about a man who is leaving his life and career in the United States to live in Rio de Janeiro with his Brazilian partner, who despite their commitment to each other was not allowed by immigration laws to stay in the states.

Perhaps you gave up a hobby to spend more time with your beloved. I remember reading several years ago that a well-known actor had liquidated his valuable comic book collection to satisfy his new wife. (Only a few months later he left her because she was "too demanding" and restarted his hobby.)

Maybe you left a previous lover when you found someone you thought was better. Or you quit a bad habit. Perhaps you got rid of some jealous friends, or rearranged your schedule, or spent a lot of money on a very special gift.

We do a lot of things for love. But have you ever loved someone so much you were willing to "put your life on the line" for them? The news is filled with such stories. A father pushes a child out of the way of an oncoming car, saving the child's life but losing his own. A brother rescues his sister from drowning in the rapids of a river but succumbs to the deadly force himself. A mother starves to death in a third-world country because she gives any food she can find to her children. A husband rescues his wife and kids from a fire raging in their bedrooms but inhales too much smoke in the process. A group of airline passengers sacrifice their lives to overcome terrorists and thus prevent the deaths of hundreds of others.

We marvel at such bravery, dedication, and sacrifice. People perform these sacrificial acts because of love. They don't even consider the cost; it's an automatic reflex. In some cases, the heroes survive their efforts to put their lives on the line, and they generally explain, "I did just what anyone else would do in the same situation."

While Jesus walked the earth, preaching, teaching, performing miracles, and demonstrating how to treat others, he fell deeply in love with his companions. He loved them utterly, to the very end. He demonstrated his love by washing their feet . . . and then suffering and dying on the cross.

We can't do more than that for love.

You too are Jesus' dear friend. You are one of the beloved companions he will love to the very end. Love one another. Put others before yourself. It's what Jesus did for his friends, for you and for me. It is the way that leads to joy, and it is the best way to love.

So, what will you do for love today?

✻ *Jesus, your love for me overwhelms me—the depth and breadth of it, the extent to which you lived it out. How do I respond to that love today? Who shall I share it with? What will I do with it? Show me. Make your joy mine in the process, whatever the cost might be.*

eighty-one

IN THE LOOP

Jesus said, "You are my friends when you do the things I command you. I'm no longer calling you servants because servants don't understand what their master is thinking and planning. No, I've named you friends because I've let you in on everything I've heard from the Father." (John 15:14–15)

When I was in junior high school, some of my good buddies and I formed a little club called the Grade Corps. Sounds very noble, doesn't it? We were all good students—geeks, actually. But we decided, why not pool our resources and make life a little easier? So we'd split up the homework every night and then secretly share the responses with each other. Actually, that practice only lasted a week or two, but we joked about the Grade Corps for years afterward.

Most of us want to belong, to be part of a group, especially the in-group. As kids we form secret clubs and build treehouse meeting places and create secret handshakes and secret codes. As teens we join cliques that outsiders cannot penetrate. Many adults join special organizations that do some civic good but also have, well, secret handshakes and secret codes. In the 2004 presidential campaign, much was made of the fact that both the incumbent and his Democratic rival were members of the ultra-secret Skull and Bones Club at Yale University, whose members were sworn to secrecy regarding the purpose and activities of the club. We like to be in on the secret things—in the select group that knows the "real truth," who are in the know behind the scenes.

Guess what? As friends of Jesus, we are in the most intimate group possible. Jesus tells his disciples—and us—that he has let us in on everything he's heard from the Father. From God's mouth to our ears.

Yes, we're to obey Jesus' commands. But that doesn't mean we're servants, instructed to carry out any order, no questions asked. No, Jesus says he trusts us with the total scoop. We understand what the Father's up to in this world, and it's all about love. Loving the other person, no matter who they are. Welcoming them into the family without reservation or hesitation.

Jesus says his friends live out of his love, carrying that love with them wherever they go, sharing it with all they meet. That means, if you're his friend you're part of the most intimate in-group ever. But it's an in-group all are welcome to join.

❋ *Jesus, thank you for trusting me enough to open the truth to me, to entrust me with all that's good, to give me your love that must be in turn given away. I want to live in a way that honors your commitment to me and opens the way to others to join us.*

eighty-two

SUFFERING THE CONSEQUENCES

> Jesus said, "If you find the godless world is hating you, remember it got its start hating me. If you lived on the world's terms, the world would love you as one of its own. But since I picked you to live on God's terms and no longer on the world's terms, the world is going to hate you." (John 15:18–19)

I don't know about you, but I prefer to be liked. Most people, I think, consider me an amiable, good-natured, easygoing, friendly, and positive guy. A few know more fully the reality of who I am, the "real me"—and a few of those still somehow like me, if not love me. Even so, I try to get along with others. Not make too many waves. Make everybody happy.

This is the sure road to impossibility—if not insanity. The older I get, the more I understand that. I think.

Jesus doesn't pull his punch here. He says if we live on God's terms, the world is simply going to hate us. Just like they hated him.

Follow the news and culture and you'll sense that a good number of Christians provoke an attitude of hatred. Sadly, many Christians deserve it. Their attitude toward certain views or people is negative and shunning, if not downright hateful. They don't live out of Jesus' love. They don't seem willing to follow his example of sacrificial love and humble service. They just want to pick a fight and demand their way.

No wonder the world hates them. But are they doing what Jesus is talking about here? Are they doing what Jesus did? I don't think so. While Jesus confronted the status quo and demanded obedience to God, he ultimately stood silently before his accusers and humbly sacrificed his own life in the face of their hatred.

On the other extreme are Christians who are indistinguishable from their worldly counterparts. They live just as selfishly as anyone. Their lives are consumed by their own interests rather than by trying to serve the needs of others. They don't give much, pray much, or do much at all. The world doesn't hate them. In fact, the world hardly even notices them; they're just part of the typical wallpaper of human life.

Jesus calls us to live somewhere between these two extremes. He calls us to live as he lived, to love as he loved, to serve as he served—and to expect to suffer the consequences.

Where are you in the continuum of worldly hatred? Is Jesus there with you?

❋ *Jesus, I admit I rarely sense the world's hatred because of the way I live or the words I say. Once again you challenge me to move out of my comfort zone, to risk saying or doing something that may get me into trouble with the world. But I know you will be there with me.*

eighty-three

ONE BY ONE

Raising his eyes in prayer, Jesus said:
"The goal is for all of them to become one heart and mind—
Just as you, Father, are in me and I in you,
So they might be one heart and mind with us.
Then the world might believe that you, in fact, sent me.
The same glory you gave me, I gave them,
So they'll be as unified and together as we are—
I in them and you in me.
Then they'll be mature in this oneness,
And give the godless world evidence

That you've sent me and loved them
In the same way you've loved me." (John 17:21–23)

The denomination I belong to, like several others, has recently been experiencing a clear—and painful—difference of opinion over an extremely difficult issue. As a result, a substantial number of clergy and members have formed an organizational structure to try to work outside the national church. Some clergy, individuals, and entire congregations have left the denomination over the issue.

Ours is hardly the only church group dealing with disagreements and potential splits. Whatever the issue may be, beliefs can be held so strongly as to cause major ruptures in churches and denominations of whatever theological stripe. Church history bears ample witness to that fact.

At the same time, exciting things are happening on an ecumenical level. For six decades the organization I work for has provided a platform for a number of denominations to work together to proclaim the good news of Jesus Christ. A vibrant organization has been formed nationally to bring together a range of Christian denominations in order to create joint efforts of ministry and witness. Another growing organization brings together a variety of faith groups to produce and distribute effective television and Internet programs and motion pictures that promote faith in God.

Does that mean there's hope for unity, for being one heart and mind together, just as Jesus and the Father are? I don't know. That seems so far away at times. Trying to get large, hierarchical church structures to get along internally—let alone with other hierarchical church structures of various sizes—seems an impossible proposition. But Jesus prayed for unity, for mature, loving oneness in the body. Perhaps he is reminding us that the body of Christ is made up of individuals. Each one has been given the glory of God, the same glory the Father gave Jesus. Each one struggles for maturity and authenticity with Jesus. Each one experiences the love Jesus has for us and discovers the calling he has issued to us.

Unity starts with one person, in relationship with Jesus, being formed into his image, maturing in faith, reaching out to another. One by one. In the love of Jesus. And the purpose? To "give the godless world evidence that you've sent me and loved them in the same way you've loved me."

Whether we recognize it or not, we are all unified in Christ's love. We are all together in this, one heart and one mind with Jesus, called to share his love with the world around us. We just don't realize it; we don't even think to live that way. Why not try to, just for today?

❋ *Jesus, I often get caught up in the disagreements and see things as black-and-white. Help me to sense my unity to all others in the body of Christ, the unity that's based on your love. And help me to live out of that unity today.*

eighty-four

EXTENDED FAMILY

> Jesus' mother, his aunt, Mary the wife of Clopas, and Mary Magdalene stood at the foot of the cross. Jesus saw his mother and the disciple he loved standing near her. He said to his mother, "Woman, here is your son." Then to the disciple, "Here is your mother." From that moment the disciple accepted her as his own mother. (John 19:25–27)

Jesus brings people together. He puts us into families for strength and comfort and encouragement and love. Here John gains a new mother, and Jesus' own mother accepts the young man she has come to know as her own son. They will care for each other for the rest of their lives.

I think of the people I have come to cherish because we enjoy mutual care and love:

- ❧ The new big brothers in New York City, Durban, South Africa, and Atlanta who are such willing listeners and share so deeply of their wisdom and love.
- ❧ The new mothers in Dallas, who, during my seminary days, took me and my young family into their hearts when we were far away from our own families.
- ❧ The new sister I met at a religious communicators meeting who has become a dear friend, willing to offer support, wisdom, and mercy through difficult times.
- ❧ The new brother from another country who has given me great joy as I've tried to help him learn English, as I've learned far more about life in all its diversity.

So many! It's a huge, extended family, tied together by Jesus' love for us and ours for one another.

Sometimes the relationships Jesus forges for us are unexpected. I find myself close to so many folks today who, years ago, I would have shunned or at least been disinterested in. Yet I discover new depths of love and joy in exploring our differences.

Who has Jesus given to you to care for? Or to be cared for by? Don't miss these God-given opportunities to expand your own family of love.

❋ *Jesus, this touching story moves me. Even as you die on the cross, your concern for those you love is preeminent. It drives you and moves you to bring us together. Help me to catch a sense of that, to live it out with those you've called to be in relationship to me. Thank you for the many wonderful parents, brothers, sisters, sons, and daughters you've given me in the faith.*

eighty-five
WIDE OPEN

Early in the morning on the first day of the week, while it was still dark, Mary Magdalene came to the tomb and saw that the stone was moved away from the entrance. She ran at once to Simon Peter and the other disciple, the one Jesus loved, breathlessly panting, "They took the Master from the tomb. We don't know where they've put him." (John 20:1–2)

Day one. Sunday. Resurrection day. The first day of a new way of life. Yet Jesus' friends don't even realize it. It is still dark when Mary Magdalene leaves her house. The sun is not yet up, although, unknown to her, the Son is.

The eastern sky is just beginning to brighten, but Mary doesn't want to wait any longer. The other women would join her shortly to care for the corpse of their beloved Master. The coming of the Sabbath had forced them to cut short their burial preparations. They could hardly bear to leave his body in the tomb. So now, very early, at the first possible moment, they return to him to finish their work.

But someone has moved the stone. The tomb's doorway is open. Wide open. Has someone disturbed Jesus' body? Or worse, taken it away for some horrible reason?

A quick look inside, in the darkness, and Mary realizes the truth: Jesus is gone. Quickly, she runs to Peter, who, despite his earlier denials of Christ, is still considered the leader of the band. John is with him. Mary blurts the awful news to them: Jesus' body has been stolen from the tomb! Who could have done it? Where could they have taken him?

Panic. Fear. Revulsion. Grief. Confusion. All rolled into one.

When the unexpected hits you, what do you do? Where do you turn? To your loved ones? Your brothers and sisters in the Spirit?

Mary did.

Together with your family of faith, you can discover the wonder of God working out the holy will that can break through our routine in astonishing ways. You can be with each other, support each other, trust each other, hold each other, and accept what God is doing in your midst. And go forward from there together.

You've probably already experienced this in many ways. In the aftermath of 9/11, churches overflowed with grieving, hurting, frightened people seeking hope and support from each other. But on a more personal scale, when some unexpected event hits home—the loss of a loved one, bad news from a doctor, the termination of a job—one of the first places I turn to is church.

In the midst of the family of faith, resurrections happen.

✠ *Jesus, where have you gone? The unthinkable has happened. Your body is missing. What could possibly have happened? Who can I turn to? I will turn to my family of faith for support, for insight, for strength. We will get through this. We will trust God together. We will gain strength from each other. No matter what the shock of life is that I may face today, help me to turn to you and to my brothers and sisters in faith.*

eighty-six

A NEW RELATIONSHIP

Jesus said, "Don't cling to me, for I have not yet ascended to the Father. Go to my brothers and tell them, 'I ascend to my Father and your Father, my God and your God.'"

Mary Magdalene went, telling the news to the disciples: "I saw the Master!" And she told them everything he said to her. (John 20:17–18)

All that Jesus had promised and more has been fulfilled: He is alive! Mary Magdalene lingered outside the empty tomb, weeping, trying to make sense of it all—until Jesus revealed himself to her. Then immediately, she fell on him, embracing him. But he tells her not to cling to him, not to hold on to him. Something is new in their relationship. It is different. He is for all to embrace—an embrace beyond the physical.

Jesus wants Mary to go to the disciples and tell them he's ascending to heaven, to the Father. But notice what he calls them. Not friends, not companions or disciples or followers. He calls them "brothers." Instead of speaking of his Father, his God, he reveals that, as brothers, he is going to their Father, their God, as well. Jesus' resurrection created a new relationship between him and his followers. All of us are now welcome to enter into brotherhood and sisterhood with Jesus himself. Anyone can be in a direct relationship with him, as family, as children of the Father.

Christ's death and resurrection make this new relationship possible. He has set things right, opened the way to new, intimate relationship, one far more intimate than the physical embrace between humans, one that is lived out beyond the surface of physical life to the eternal life of the soul.

More and more people can enter into this relationship as we reach out to them with the love that forges it. This is the spiritual embrace of those connected at the soul, and all are welcome to share it. Including you.

❋ *Jesus, thank you for opening the way for me to be your sibling in the deepest, richest sense of the word. Thank you for giving me the opportunity to live in the most intimate relationship with you, Risen Lord, forever. And to share that relationship with others.*

eighty-seven

WORDS TO LIVE BY

> Later on that day, the disciples had gathered together, but, fearful of the Jews, had locked all the doors in the house. Jesus entered, stood among them, and said, "Peace to you." Then he showed them his hands and side.
>
> The disciples, seeing the Master with their own eyes, were exuberant. Jesus repeated his greeting: "Peace to you. Just as the Father sent me, I send you."
>
> Then he took a deep breath and breathed into them. "Receive the Holy Spirit," he said. (John 20:19–22)

Put yourself in the disciples' place. All of you—except Judas—are together in a locked room, still reeling over the death of your beloved teacher and fearful of the outside world and the uproar your Master has caused.

All of a sudden, the risen Lord somehow enters the room, even though the door is locked. He stands with you, offers you perfect peace, and validates his identity by showing you the marks of cruel death his resurrected body still bears.

As you stand there, excited and joyful, he says three things to you:

- *Peace to you.* He knows the emotional turmoil you've been jerked by—from the extreme sadness, fear, and shame to the exuberant joy of his resurrection. He is saying he is present and will be present with you, if you will open yourself up to him. When you sense his presence, you will have peace. The surface may be chaotic at times, but deep down, peace will run through your heart like a strong, sure stream.
- *Just as the Father sent me, I send you.* This is big. After all, the Father sent Jesus to show the world how much God loves each person, living among them, serving them, heal-

ing them, teaching them, performing miracles among them, reconciling them to one another, sacrificing for them—even to death. Now Jesus is sending you on the same mission.

Receive the Holy Spirit. Jesus is not leaving you alone with your own resources to fulfill this mission. He takes a deep breath and breathes into your very being the Holy Spirit, God's living and active presence, the Guide and Sustainer of your life. It's a holy mouth-to-mouth resuscitation. It's as though Jesus himself is now within you, empowering you and filling you with everything you need to live joyfully and to serve lovingly.

Let Jesus' words sink into your deepest self. Receive them. Believe them. Live them. Share them.

Jesus, thank you for your living and powerful presence in my life, thank you for your peace, and thank you for the Holy Spirit dwelling within me. What wonderful gifts these are! And how little I deserve them. Help me to put them to good use for your sake.

eighty-eight

JUMPING IN

Simon Peter announced, "I'm going fishing."

The rest of them replied, "We're going with you." They went out and got in the boat. They caught nothing that night. When the sun came up, Jesus was standing on the beach, but they didn't recognize him.

Jesus spoke to them: "Good morning! Did you catch anything for breakfast?"

They answered, "No."

He said, "Throw the net off the right side of the boat and see what happens."

They did what he said. All of a sudden there were so many fish in it, they weren't strong enough to pull it in.

> Then the disciple Jesus loved said to Peter, "It's the Master!"
> When Simon Peter realized that it was the Master, he threw on some clothes, for he was stripped for work, and dove into the sea. (John 21:3–7)

Was it the words Jesus said? The warm chuckle in his voice? The love that emanated from the shoreline, clear out to the boat? What was it that clicked in the mind of "the disciple Jesus loved" when he peered at the stranger calling to them from the lakeside?

It's fitting that John, the one who had the deepest, closest friendship with Jesus, recognizes him first. John, the one who was always with Jesus in the most amazing times of his ministry. The one who lay against him at the Passover banquet in the upper room, his head serenely, comfortably resting on his friend's heart. The one who became Mary's new son, urged by his dying friend to care for her and love her as his mother. The one who, just maybe, knew Jesus best. Or the one who felt most known by Jesus.

No wonder John immediately knew who the stranger was. "It's the Master!"

He's your Master too.

Your Lord, your friend, the lover of your soul calls to you from the shore. Do you see him? Do you recognize him? Do you know him? Do you hear what he is calling you to do?

Jump in!

❋ *Jesus, thank you that you want me to see, recognize, and know you, because you love me. Thank you for calling to me, for being with me. Thank you that I don't have to keep you to myself, but that all God's children are your beloved and that we can share your presence with one another.*

eighty-nine

FEEDING SHEEP

> Then Jesus said it a third time: "Simon, son of John, do you love me?"
>
> Peter was upset that he asked for the third time, "Do you love me?" so he answered, "Master, you know everything there is to know. You've got to know that I love you."
>
> Jesus said, "Feed my sheep." . . . And then he commanded, "Follow me." (John 21:17–19)

Jesus didn't ask Peter three times, "Do you love me?" because he didn't know the answer to the question or because he needed emotional reassurance from Peter. He knew Peter loved him. Jesus was reminding Peter that he indeed loved Jesus, even though the disciple had denied that love three times on the night of Jesus' arrest.

Peter must have felt uncomfortable and ashamed of what he had done. But the shame wasn't coming from Jesus. Jesus wanted to reconnect with him—to clear up the anxious strain that Peter had imposed on the relationship. Jesus was restoring Peter to full relationship with him, because Peter was the one who had turned his back on his friend.

As Peter acknowledged, Jesus knows everything there is to know, which means he knows everything there is to know about you. Jesus is aware of every nuance of your feelings about life, about your faith, about himself. He knows you love him, although sometimes that love may be clouded by fear or grief, or ignored because of various distractions, good and bad.

Jesus knows that you love him, no matter what. He challenges you, like Peter, to live out of that love. Not to keep it to yourself, not to hoard it, not to focus on how it meets your needs for comfort and intimacy, but to reach out and share it. To "feed my sheep" in service and witness and compassion. To follow him. To let his example of sacrificial, loving care—healing, teaching, guiding, challenging all those he came in contact with—guide you into a fulfilling life of service in his name.

Is there a strain between you and Jesus right now, some guilt on your part that makes it hard for you to look your loving, forgiving Master in the eyes?

Listen to Jesus speak to you. Sense his faithful love to you. Hear his call to serve him.

❋ *Jesus, you know I love you. Help me to keep that love relationship open and clear of any guilt or distraction or strain. Help me to accept your challenge to feed your sheep, to follow you, to live out of your love for me.*

ninety

IN HIS HANDS

> Turning his head, Peter noticed the disciple Jesus loved following right behind. When Peter noticed him, he asked Jesus, "Master, what's going to happen to *him*?"
>
> Jesus said, "If I want him to live until I come again, what's that to you? You—follow me." (John 21:20–22)

Jesus has just told Peter that he will be a shepherd to the sheep and will die a martyr's death. He has challenged his brother, friend, and disciple with "Follow me"—follow his example of sacrificial service, even to the death. It's only natural for Peter to ask whether the beloved John, who was there with them, would also suffer a tragic fate. It's almost as though one brother wants to know if he is going to be treated any better or worse than his sibling.

Jesus makes it clear that our lives, our fates, our futures, are totally in his hands. Life happens, but it is lived in the arms of a loving, caring Lord who knows each of us and wants the best for each of us.

Jesus also makes it clear that he has a purpose for each of our lives, a unique mission to love him and share that love in serving others. He tells Peter, again, very clearly, his purpose: "You—follow me." No ifs, ands, or buts. No dawdling. No questions.

Jesus will guide each of us into the purpose, calling, and mission he has for us. He will walk with us in it every step of the way. He reminds us not to be distracted when someone else seems to get the better deal, when someone else apparently receives more blessings or honor in life. "What's that to you?"

Know that Jesus loves you, understands what's best for you, and is with you in the long process of becoming all you have been created to be in him.

Rest in that truth. It can set you free to live your life more meaningfully and to fulfill your calling to share his love.

❋ *Jesus, I put my life in your hands. You do know what's best for me, and I know you love me utterly. Build my trust in that truth and set me free to live the life you've called me—and only me—to live.*

POSTLUDE

Just about every summer of my youth, my family spent a month at the beach on the James River in Virginia. It was the place I described earlier in the chapter "Storm-Tossed Glory"—the place decimated by a hurricane a few years ago.

Sunken Meadow Beach got its name from an adjacent meadow full of cypress trees that had been flooded and filled with river water many years earlier. It was my father's favorite fishing place. (Later it was renamed Sunny Meadow Beach in a misguided effort at PR-style positiveness, but my family to this day only uses that name derisively.) We'd spend that summer month in a ramshackle, two-bedroom, screen-porched cabin. I can still smell the piney cleanser the cleaning people used so liberally to scour the apartment after the last folks left and before we moved in for the month. It's a smell that still holds for me the magic of summer expectations, a bittersweet aroma.

Each year I hoped and prayed for a summer romance at Sunken Meadow Beach. Maybe I would meet a cute girl to have some fun with, maybe to be pen pals with after we returned home. Or find a new best buddy to explore the clay banks and secret coves with. Someone to hang out with other than my little sister—please, God!

But each summer that dream for love proved elusive, that prayer unanswered. So I'd spend time with my family, including some aunts and uncles and cousins, swimming in the river, touring beautiful areas of Tidewater Virginia, playing every manner of card game, or just sitting and talking. I'd get letters from my buddies back home, sharing the latest gossip, asking me if I'd had a chance to pick up the new issue of *Spider-Man,* and generally just goofing around with pen on paper.

In hindsight, I can see I was bathed in love from all sides during those long summer days. But I had in my mind what that love was supposed to look like and who it was supposed to involve, so I rarely acknowledged or experienced the love that abounded so richly.

Sometimes I still have that problem. Maybe you can identify with me. I want to live loved, and sometimes I still search for Jesus' love. Sometimes this search brings wonderful insights and experiences, surprising opportunities to be stretched in service to others. Sometimes I can really, truly feel the Savior's warm embrace—almost physically. Once, on a retreat I made during Lent at a North Georgia conference center, as I read Scripture after Scripture about God's love and calling on us all, I began to weep. I felt a sense of acceptance I never had felt before. It was as if Jesus were literally embracing me, holding me close to his heart.

Other times, I just keep searching for his love. Sometimes that search doesn't feel like it produces any results. But maybe that's because I'm looking for it in the wrong way, for the wrong reasons, from the wrong person. My expectations have blinded me to the reality that is there, always there, surrounding us with love.

A year or so ago I visited a friend in Chicago. On a brisk, crystal-clear day, we drove along Lake Michigan near Wilmette, and I spotted the Baha'i Temple looming over the autumn-leafed trees. My friend suggested we go visit. As we entered the intricately designed dome, I saw an inscription over the door: "My love is My stronghold; he that entereth therein is safe and secure." It was a powerful reminder that stays with me to this day.

I hope that in the process of reading this book you've come to know beyond a doubt that Jesus loves you. Like me, you may not have all the answers, but you do know you are loved. You've chosen to enter into his love and have found it a stronghold. And you've learned to experience his love in unexpected ways and to share it as liberally as he does.

We can live our life in darkness and doubt, battered by the winds of the world, constantly striving to find what we think will calm things down and give us peace. Or we can live it knowing we are loved, seeking to know and experience and share that love relentlessly.

This way of life is not easy. You will realize that just by looking at Jesus' life and at the lives of those who have known him and loved him and followed him no matter what, often to their deaths. But it is the way of the loved.

The truth is, we are loved whether we know it or experience it or share it. But how much richer life can be when we are alive to that love, when we seek it, open our eyes and hearts to it, shatter our expectations of it, and welcome it without hesitation.

There is light ahead. It is the light of freedom, of truth, of love. I am heading toward it, step by step. I hope you are with me on that journey.

I know Jesus is.

NOTES

1. "Hoffman's Attention to Detail," *The Week* (December 10, 2004): 10.
2. Tom Wright, *John for Everyone: Part One (Chapters 1–10)* (London: SPCK, 2002), x.
3. Peter Wallace, *Out of the Quiet: Responding to God's Whispered Invitations* (Colorado Springs: NavPress, 2004), 7.
4. William Blake, *Poems and Prophecies* (New York: Dutton, 1970), 10. Quoted by Gerald May, *The Awakened Heart* (San Francisco: HarperSanFrancisco, 1993), 1.
5. Gerald May, from the epilogue in *Holy Meeting Ground.* Used with the permission of the Shalem Institute, Bethesda, Md.; www.shalem.org.
6. Barbara Brown Taylor, "Truth to Tell" in "The Perfect Mirror," *The Christian Century* (March 18–25, 1998).
7. Daniel Ladinsky, trans., *Love Poems from God: Twelve Sacred Voices from the East and West* (New York: Penguin Compass, 2002), 45. Used by permission.
8. Ladinsky, *Love Poems from God,* 186. Used by permission.
9. Thich Nhat Hanh, *Living Buddha, Living Christ* (New York: Riverhead Books, 1995), 30.
10. Henri Nouwen, *The Inner Voice of Love* (New York: Doubleday, 1996), 47–48. Used by permission of Doubleday, a division of Random House.
11. Thomas R. Hatina, "'That They May Be One': Love in St. John and Vladimir Soloviev," *The Anglican Catholic* 15 (Summer 2003): 19–20.
12. Nouwen, *Inner Voice of Love,* 40–41. Used by permission.
13. Don Plummer, "Brutal Crime, Then Forgiveness," *Atlanta Journal-Constitution* (November 17, 2004), B3.
14. Wright, *John for Everyone: Part One*, 113.
15. Tom Wright, *John for Everyone: Part Two (Chapters 11–21)* (London: SPCK, 2002), 10–11. Emphasis in original.
16. Brennan Manning, *The Rabbi's Heartbeat* (Colorado Springs: NavPress, 2003), 96–97.
17. Prayer 251 in the service for Evening Prayer (Vespers), *Lutheran Book of Worship* (Minneapolis: Augsburg, 1978), 153.
18. Henri J. M. Nouwen, quoted in *Living With Christ* (January 2004): 163.

ABOUT THE AUTHOR

Peter Marsden Wallace is the host and executive producer of *Day1* (formerly *The Protestant Hour*), an ecumenical, weekly radio program airing on more than 160 stations and online (www.Day1.net). He earned a bachelor's degree in journalism from Marshall University in Huntington, West Virginia, and a Master of Theology from Dallas Theological Seminary.

Peter served as editorial director for Walk Thru the Bible Ministries from 1984 to 1990, then was senior copywriter for Larry Smith & Associates Advertising in Atlanta for eleven years before joining *The Protestant Hour* organization in March 2001. He is also vice-president of production for the Alliance for Christian Media, the parent organization of the *Day1* ministry.

He is the author of several books, including *Out of the Quiet: Responding to God's Whispered Invitations* (NavPress) and *TruthQuest Devotional Journal* (Broadman & Holman). He has contributed to many books, study Bibles, devotional guides, magazines, teaching curricula, and other resources. An Episcopalian, he lives in Atlanta and has two grown children and two grandchildren.